# THE LUCKY LIFE

## The Backwards Beatitudes

By

## Skip Moen, D. Phil.

This book is dedicated to Luzette and Erika whose unrelenting encouragement to finish the manuscript sitting dormant on my computer lead to this humble attempt to uncover the depth of Yeshua's thought.

Sterkte!

zhù nǐ háoyùn

Held og lykke!

Bonne chance !

Alles Gute!

בהצלחה

Buona fortuna!

Bona fortuna!

Καλή τύχη!

Амжилт хүсье

¡Buena suerte!

Suwertehin ka sana

Zol zayn mit mazl!

Ngikufisela iwela!

**GOOD LUCK!**

# *T*able of *C*ontents

# The Backwards Beatitudes

**Luck is for losers.** Winners do not believe in luck. But they do believe in the **lucky life**. They believe in the lucky life because God's view of life is all about being lucky. Understanding the difference between luck and lucky will change everything.

Stop waiting for good luck! Start living the lucky life – the life God designed.

In 2002 my luck ran out. In a single e-mail, I discovered that I was the victim of a huge financial fraud. My wife and I lost all our liquid assets in one day. We went from millionaires to paupers at the speed of the Internet. That's when God introduced me to the life of a man named Job. That's when I began to learn something about the difference between luck and lucky. Today I have not recovered from this financial blow. I will never see that money again. But my life is far richer because I know now what it really means to be lucky. I don't need good luck. I don't even want it. Good luck is a myth of the "accidental" world. What I want is the lucky life God tells me that I can have. And He *guarantees* it. Living according to His design means my good luck will never run out.

When life smacks you in the face, when the only kind of luck you have is bad luck, it's time to change your point of view. Luck is for losers. Now it's time to let God show you the lucky life He wants for you.

# $\mathcal{L}$ife As It Is: $\mathcal{T}$he Biggest Lottery on Earth

Would you play the lottery if you were guaranteed to win?

According to current surveys, today more people believe that they will become millionaires by winning the lottery than by developing a business or working hard at what they do. That's why they play. They want to win big. They want to put life's problems behind them and be free from worry. However, it shouldn't surprise us that most people who win the lottery are broke within a few years. Winning the lottery changed the size of the bank account but it did not change the kind of person who signed the checks. The old habits just got bigger budgets.

God has a lottery too. The difference is that God has designed His lottery so that everyone can win – and keep the winnings. That's what Yeshua[1] tried to tell us in those famous sayings on the hillside. The Beatitudes are not spiritual exercises. They are not a new kind of morality. *They are lottery tickets in the biggest game.* The best part about this lottery is that everyone who gets a ticket wins the jackpot. There is no limit in God's lottery. Forget Pick 6 or Scratch Off. If you play in God's lottery, you will win the big one – Life the way it's supposed to be.

How do you play God's lottery of life? Amazingly, in this lottery you don't even have to buy a ticket. Just being alive makes you a player. God tells us that if

---

[1] Yeshua is the proper name of the man most of us call "Jesus." He is a Jew and His name is Jewish, so in this book, I will use the name He was given, not the one we gave Him.

you play the game His way, you win. If you try to play the game your way, you are guaranteed to lose. No amount of *luck* will make any difference to the outcome. If you want to win, you need to listen to what Yeshua says about this game. He gives us the "How to Play" manual for the Lucky Life. The only question is this: are we willing to play His way?

The Beatitudes don't sound like fortunes from Chinese cookies. They sound like disasters. Poor, mourning, hungry, dirty, guilty and persecuted; those aren't the kind of words that we associate with lucky. That's the mystery of the Beatitudes. They are sacred paradoxes about the lucky life. When you discover what they really say, you can't help shouting, "WOW! I just won God's prize." Put aside all those old Sunday school lessons on the Beatitudes. Push away your preconceived ideas about being a good person or living up to the rules. The Beatitudes are not about how to become more virtuous. The Beatitudes are about responding to life *as it is*. They are God's view of what it means to be lucky. When life throws curve balls or hits below the belt, Yeshua says, "Now you are playing in God's lottery. Now you are the lucky one. Jump for joy. You win."

Oswald Chambers' thoughts were collected into the most popular daily devotional ever printed. His comments for May 26 ask us to take Yeshua at his word and live life accordingly. Chambers says:

> The danger with us is that we want to water down the things that Jesus says and make them mean something in accordance with common sense; if it were only common sense, it was not worthwhile for Him to say it.[2]

---

[2] Oswald Chambers, *My Utmost For his Highest*, (Barbour & Company), 1935, p. 147.

3

I believe that this is what we have done with those statements Yeshua made on the hillside – the statements that we call "the Beatitudes". We have tried to make Yeshua's words into comments about economic, political or material well-being. We don't need a Yeshua who is "politically correct," so we have focused on the "spiritual" meanings of these verses. But even these efforts have converted the words of Yeshua into common sense "God" language. We have diluted His declarations to accommodate our contemporary religious pluralism and our Greek metaphysical views. If all that Yeshua provided was another set of religious principles or prosperity formulae, then He will have given us nothing truly profound. For example, it is patently obvious that mercy should flow to those who show mercy. But Yeshua cannot be that shallow.

When I study these short sentences carefully, when I begin to understand the deeper meanings of the Greek words and their Hebrew backgrounds, I find something very different than contemporary treatments of the Beatitudes as "religious" blessings. I find a radical, upside down, backwards thinking about life that says that my usual commonsense view is not even close to what God thinks. The Beatitudes are suddenly converted from spiritual comments on proper attitudes into penetrating, demanding and incredibly revealing looks into a kingdom that is nearly invisible to the commonsense eye. The Beatitudes become proclamations of the destruction of my commonsense values. These "macarisms" (that's really what they are – a particular pattern of sayings that come from the first word of each statement in the Greek – *makarios*) show that Yeshua was greater than any Zen master who ever lived. In less than a dozen sentences, he completely undoes the world's values and goals by showing us that the

4

Ruler of the Universe has a radically different perspective about those who are "jumping for joy."

Read on and see for yourself. You'll never be able to listen to a "Blessed are" again without wanting to stand on your head.

# The Sacred Paradoxes

Before we discover the "jump for joy" news of the Beatitudes, we need to get an overview of the entire section in Mathew.[3]

Many writers have taken up the task of interpreting the Beatitudes. After all, these are probably some of the most memorized and quoted words of Yeshua. The treatment of these verses covers the gamut, from Swartz (*The Magnificent Obsession*) and Lucado (*The Applause of Heaven*) to the commentaries of Nicoll and Robinson to the linguistic studies in the *Theological Dictionary of the New Testament*. All excellent, all different. Swartz and Lucado present the Beatitudes in the context of the gospel message. Commentators usually attempt to place the words in the framework of the ethics of the Kingdom of God. The *Theological Dictionary of the New Testament* (TDNT) does not comment on the Beatitudes as such but rather on the individual words within these verses and the wider theological implications. Nearly every theologian of the New Testament, and most preachers of the Gospel have written or spoken about these words. There is no lack of material for the student. The question is whether or not we have learned anything truly penetrating.

As I read the authors mentioned above and many more, I find much that is comforting, powerful, insightful and intense. But I also find something missing. It's not that I think these authors and great scholars are wrong. Not at all. It's just that what I

---

[3] This study follows the Beatitudes in the Gospel of Matthew, chapter 5. The alternate recording of these statements is found in the Gospel of Luke, chapter 6. This alternate presents some special exegetical problems that I discuss in Appendix 1.

miss is the shock value that Yeshua's words have. After twenty centuries of spiritualization, I am afraid that most of these verses have become so familiar that we forget just how disturbing these words were to the audience that heard them first. It's certainly true that Yeshua knew He was speaking words for the ages. But first and foremost, He was teaching the assembly of fellow-countrymen who sat at His feet on that day two thousand years ago. If we don't understand what these words meant for them, then we miss something important. In fact, we might even miss the deepest meanings of these proclamations. If we don't realize that Yeshua speaks within the continuity of rabbinic expression of that time, we will miss the context. We will elevate Yeshua's remarks to spiritual mantras and go off proclaiming that they are magical pathways to greater goodness or carefully disguised steps in the plan of salvation. We will end up treating these remarks as though they were not spoken by a Jewish theologian to Jewish disciples in an occupied Jewish country.

This need for critical context is exemplified in the first word of every statement: *makarios* – the Greek word that we usually translate "Blessed". As we shall see, it really means something quite different than "blessed". The use of this Greek word announces something important beyond its literal meaning. It tells us that these sayings are part of a stylistic pattern that first appeared in the poet Pindar about 500BC. The style became so popular that it was known as a *macarism* (a blessing). Although the word began as a poetic form designating the state of blissful release from our earthly life of trouble and toil, it soon became a description of the favorable action of the Greek gods. By the time Aristotle used the word, it no longer signified only religious blessing. It became a stylized saying of the common language of men, proclaiming happy release from the sorrows of normal life.

For the Greeks, there was no connection to a heavenly personal God. A macarism was a pithy expression of happiness related to the values of this world. One example is "He who has no possessions is free of many worries". We have the same sort of literature in the famous sayings of Benjamin Franklin: "Early to bed and early to rise" or "A stitch in time". For the Greeks, these sayings were about children, wealth, love, honor and fame. The content is not crucial to us. It is the pattern that is important. That pattern extols good fortune and release from the world's troubles, either through earthly gains or inner peace and piety. Macarisms offered general advice about living by pointing out those who would receive favorable status in this life. Macarisms are the Greek equivalent of sayings that describe the paradoxes of life.

The same pattern of blessing can be found in the Old Testament wisdom literature. "Blessed is he who trusts in the name of the Lord" and "Blessed is he whose sins are forgiven" are examples. These are sayings of practical wisdom with deep spiritual connections.[4] But these patterns in Hebrew are not quite the same as their Greek counterparts because the Hebrew perspective on life is not the same as the Greek worldview. Consequently, in spite of the fact that our Greek text uses the pattern of a macarism, we must be exceedingly careful not to adopt the Greek meaning without a long look in the direction of the Hebrew sages. As we shall see, the use of *makarios* is laden with Hebrew thought antedating even the Greek patterns. There is something

---

[4] For a complete list of every use of *makarios* in the Old and New Testament, see Appendix 2

happening here that will escape us if we are not careful.

Our English translations used the word "blessed" for two different Hebrew words. The meanings of these two words are distinctly different. The first is *barak*. If we wanted a Hebrew word that carried the idea of receiving a blessing from someone in authority, this would be the word. It is a verb that means, "to bless, kneel, salute or greet." This word specifically includes the concept of passing a favor from one person to another, and particularly from God to men. It is found hundreds of times in the Old Testament. But it is not the word that is associated with the Old Testament's version of a macarism. The word translated *makarios* in Greek is the Hebrew word *ashrei*.[5] It is a noun (not a verb) that describes a person's *state of being*. This word is often used to describe the inner state of a man or an entire nation that enjoys fellowship with God. It is never used to describe God's state of being. The distinction is important. God is not blessed in this sense because God lacks nothing for His own state of well-being. But a man can be blessed when *his own actions* bring about a state of well-being. The word *ashrei* announces good fortune or congratulations to a man whose inner state is blissful. In Hebrew, this is not the result of a "blessing", a gift granted by someone in authority. *It is the result of actions that I take on my own.* My decisions and behavior determine whether I enjoy inner bliss or not. This is fundamental to the idea expressed in Yeshua's Beatitudes. These sayings are not about magical means for obtaining God's favors. They are about the *inner bliss* of those who participate in actions that

---

[5] There are many examples of this translation in the Septuagint. See in particular Ps. 1:1, 32:1 and 2, 40:4, 41:1, 65:4, 84:4 and 5, 94:12, 119:1 and 2, and 128:1.

express God's character.   The Beatitudes are not spiritual formulae for temporal or eternal good fortune.  They are *present descriptions* of the kind of person who experiences something about God's character.

*ashrei* is the word that forms the Hebrew context of Yeshua's remarks.  Unlike the Greeks, the context of these blessings is within the framework of God's governance.  Even when the Old Testament blessings are about prosperity or success on this earth, they are couched  within the context of the chosen people of God.  Yeshua is describing those people whose lives are characterized by an internal bliss, an psychic state that demonstrates contentment and harmony with God's greater purposes.  These are people who understand the human dynamic of a relationship with God.  They are not strangers to God's will.  They are not pagans.  They are not the unsaved.  They enjoy God's graces because they have some inner qualities that allow God to demonstrate His presence in their lives.   The only problem with Yeshua's description is this:  the people he picks out seem to be the least likely candidates for bliss.  Everything about them says that they should be very unhappy indeed.  In other words, commonsense tells us that these people are the most miserable of all, but Yeshua turns all this upside down.

In general, a macarism has both a linguistic and an instructional pattern.  The linguistic pattern is the **announcement** of favor, **who** the announcement concerns, and a following **relative clause that explains** the reason for this happy state.   The instructional pattern is an **announcement**, a **recipient** and a **teaching** about life.

But something changed when Yeshua employed this familiar pattern.  Linguistically, Yeshua's macarisms are still announcements (not commands or magic success formulae or spiritual attitudes, by the way), but the "who" of these announcements is specified in an entirely new way. First, the "who" is plural. Secondly, the ones to whom the announcement applies are actually already hidden in the relative clause that contains the explanation. In other words, if we really understand the teaching, we will find that the linguistic pattern turns back on itself to tell us that the reason for their happiness is already contained in the characteristics of those who are part of the announcement. Yeshua is explaining bliss in concise statements about what it means to be joyfully happy. He is not telling us what we must *do* to become happy. He is pointing to those whose lives are candidates for happiness because of *what and who they are*. In other words, these people are happy, lucky and even "blessed" because of who they are, not what they have done.

An example will help us see this unique feature. When we understand the meaning of the term "comforted", we will see that this concept is already contained in what Yeshua means by those who "mourn". We will find that "peacemaker" is already contained in the concept "sons of God". One concept reflects the other. Yeshua uses the second part of the thought to produce a great U turn in our thinking, driving us back to the first part of the verse in an "Ah ha!" moment. Yeshua uses this linguistic device to turn the logic of the macarism upside down. This is Hebrew instruction at its best, unpacking the meaning of simple life situations to demonstrate that "something sacred hangs in the balance of every moment" (as Abraham Heschel would say).

The teaching pattern is also revolutionary. Yeshua announces happiness to exactly those whom the world considers the unhappiest of all. His announcements about the happy ones seem *utterly paradoxical*. They are all backwards! Yeshua's macarisms reverse all of the expected values of life on earth. What commonsense says about being happy is just the opposite of what Yeshua says is real happiness.

Each of the Beatitudes introduces a class of people who seem entirely incapable of being happy. They are:

the destitute
the losers
the oppressed
the ones under judgment
the ones who don't get what they deserve
the ones who aren't good enough
the ones who put themselves at risk
the ones who are being persecuted

All of the Beatitudes focus on something that the world rejects or attempts to avoid. We can hardly imagine how anyone described in these ways could ever be a candidate for "jumping for joy" happiness. But Yeshua says they are. Yeshua tells us in his macarisms that God intends to make the wisdom of men foolishness and the foolishness of God eternal wisdom. In every case, the true reality exposes the character of God's Kingdom, not the mistaken reality of this world. Yeshua tells us that we must think backwards if we are to see God's reign.

# $\mathcal{D}$esperate

**"Blessed are the poor in spirit for theirs is the kingdom of heaven" Matthew 5:3**

Wednesday, March 26. The man from Uz stopped by to say hello.

Most of my life I feared his visit. I suspect that none of us really want him to show up at our front door. When he comes, pain and suffering follow. Of course I was afraid. But like most of his visits, I didn't know he was coming until he was already there. No longer the man of ancient times, he traveled electronically from half way around the world to greet me. Believing that my world was safe and secure, I simply opened the evening e-mails. And there he was, shaking hands with me. In a few sentences, my world collapsed. Job came to my house.

Job lived in Uz. One day, for no reason that he could imagine, four messengers arrived at his doorstep. Each one brought news of disaster. In the course of a single afternoon, Job lost everything. He was transformed from a prosperous, joyous father to a man of sorrows, acquainted with grief. His life was turned upside-down with pain and suffering.

On the Wednesday that Job greeted me, my life was shaken to the core. One minute I was a multi-millionaire, the next I was penniless. One minute I was secure in myself, the next I was completely vulnerable. One minute I had few cares and concerns, the next I was afraid. All that I thought was right with my life was gone. What fell on me was unexpected catastrophe. I was caught in the vise and my life was being squeezed from me. Suddenly my life was spelled "desperate".

Job listened to those messengers. When they finished their declarations, Job went out of his house, tore his clothes from his body, fell on his knees and said, "God! You brought me into the world with nothing. I will leave the world with nothing. You give and you take away. I will still worship you."

After I heard what Job said to me, I was so numb that I could hardly think. My security was stripped away in the blink of an eye. Everything that I thought I could count on, all the plans and hopes for my future, were dashed to pieces. I was afraid to the bottom of my soul. How could I survive? What would I do? Where could I go? Who would help me? I should have listened to Job's reply when his life turned to ashes. God gives and God takes away. The question is not what I have but whom I worship.

I sat still. Thousands of miles from my home, alone, disconnected from everything that I counted on, my chest felt as though a mountain fell on it. My stomach was sour with dread. My head hurt. My mind reeled with panic. I clenched my teeth to stay in control. Death would have been easier than this. To live with the pain, to have to bear the suffering of losing everything. To know that friends, family, loved-ones who counted on me would be pulled into this spiral. It was almost too much. The air I tried to breathe was sick syrup, choking me. Where was God? Why was this happening to me? I thought I was safe. I thought I had achieved the dream – independently wealthy. Now it was gone. And deep inside I knew why. I just didn't want to admit it or even think about it. I was not Job, the righteous man from Uz. I was Jacob, the manipulator, the schemer, the unrighteous fortune seeker. And God was hunting me down.

The Christian Church has often claimed that Yeshua was a radical. This proclamation has been particularly useful in the last few decades when the Church wished to raise the banner of social justice, political freedom or some other worthy humanitarian cause. We have seen the portraits of Yeshua as the fiery charismatic, the protector of the innocent, the liberator of the down-trodden. But I often wonder whether Yeshua himself would choose to be at the head of the parade for human causes. I often wonder whether we have not conscripted him to elevate our own moral failings, infusing them with divine authority simply because we wish to rally God's forces behind our otherwise potentially corrupted motives in order to be counted among those who do good.

Consider for a moment the truly radical nature of Yeshua's teaching in these sayings that we all memorized without much comprehension - the Beatitudes. Let us examine the first one in Matthew's version. It will be enough, perhaps more than enough, to show us that something about our own aspirations is drastically out of line. It will be enough to show us that the nature of Yeshua's declaration of the Kingdom reveals that it is more than likely not for us at all.

The first Beatitude is found in Matthew's gospel, chapter 5 verse 3. Our English translations are something akin to this, "Blessed are the poor in spirit for theirs is the kingdom of heaven". That's probably the way most of us learned the verse. Unfortunately, learning it like this has meant that most of us never really had any idea what Yeshua was actually saying.

Our first misunderstanding comes with the opening word, "Blessed". While this certainly sounds lofty, something fitting for a pronouncement from the lips of the Incarnate Christ, the actual word is not really about bestowing some great favor. The word in the text, handed down to us in a Greek translation from Hebrew, is *makarioi* (μακαριοι) and it really means "happy" or "lucky." Robertson says:

> The English word "blessed" is more exactly represented by the Greek verbal *eulogetoi* as in Luke 1:68 of God by Zacharias, or the perfect passive participle *eulogemenos* as in Luke 1:42 of Mary by Elizabeth and in Matt 21:9. Both forms come from *eulogeo*, to speak well of (*eu, logos*). The Greek word here (*makarioi*) is an adjective that means "happy" which in English etymology goes back to hap, chance, good-luck as seen in our words haply, hapless, happily, happiness.

The reason these verses are called the Beatitudes is that the translation of the first Greek word into Latin produces the Latin word *beatitudo*, which means blessing. This Latin word was transported into the English Bible without being translated. This is called *transliteration*. This produces the "blessings" of the Beatitudes.

But there may also be an ecclesiastical reason behind this transliteration. The idea of a blessing contains the thought of someone in higher authority granting a favor to someone in a lower position. From the position of God's supreme authority, blessings are *granted* to His children, just as a king *grants* favors to his subjects. The catholic church of the Roman Empire also enters into this hierarchy. "Blessed" would make us think that we are going to be given something. It would make us think that we are some special class of people who will be granted an incredible favor from the King of kings. "Blessed" makes us think that this statement is about an action of lofty, divine *entitlement*. That's because "blessed" is associated with an English word that comes from a root meaning to be marked with blood, consecrated, praised. Blessed is more in line with our thoughts about being set apart. It carries with it the notion of somehow being marked as special, of having a birthright. As we shall see, the retention of the idea of "blessed" radically affects the interpretation of this verse.

If we wanted to retain the power of the church and its priestly hierarchy over a submissive congregation, what better vehicle could we conscript than the very words of Yeshua, conveniently reinterpreted to express the granting of a gift or favor? Penitent souls come before the almighty church, doing obeisance in order to receive the blessing of their Master, duly granted by His authorized representatives. "Blessing" is a power word. Used effectively, it keeps everyone in the hierarchy in line.

But not so with a translation like "happy." The church and its representatives may claim to "grant" God's blessings, but they cannot grant "happiness". Happiness is a state that knows no hierarchy. The least in the kingdom can certainly be happier than the most powerful in the kingdom without requiring a "favor" at all. Blessing is directional and regulated. Happiness is dispersed and unregulated.

The idea found in the English word "blessed" is not at all what Yeshua was saying, not even close. In the Greek mind, when you blessed someone you gave him or her the gift of praise; you spoke well of them. But Yeshua is not implying this. Far from it. He is saying something about *luck*. Whomever he happens to be addressing in this odd statement (and we have yet to see who that might be), he is announcing that the hearer of this proclamation is lucky, fortunate, glad, happy or content. Something amazing is occurring, and the hearer is going to be the luckiest person alive just for hearing it. So, "Pay attention, audience!" says Yeshua. "What I am about to say will produce great joy, heart-throbbing, mind-leaping euphoria. If you are a hearer of this word, you have just won the lottery. God's lottery. And the prize is beyond counting. Leap for joy, your ship has come in. Be happy! You're the lucky one."

The church may wish to retain *beatitudo* in its arsenal of power, but Yeshua seems to be saying something very different. What kind of happiness is he describing?

**Playing Without A Ticket**

Newman and Stine[6] point out that nearly all English translations fail to communicate a very important element found in the opening word, *makarioi*. What we miss in our English translations is that the sense of the statement is *passive*. God is the active agent here, not the people identified by the opening word *makarioi*. There is a reason why the word is an adjective, not a verb. The action described in each of the Beatitudes is *brought upon these people*. They are the passive recipients of this bliss. They have won the lottery *without even buying a ticket*. This is a jarring observation because it stands in contrast to the Hebrew use of the word *ashrei*, the word Yeshua would have used in his Hebrew expression. If we pursue the Greek implications, we will have to

---

[6] Newman, Barclay M. and Stine, Philip C, *A Handbook on The Gospel of Matthew* (United Bible Societies, New York), 1988, p. 107.

reconcile this dilemma. That will be done, but first we must see what a mess this makes for the English reader.

Here we must be very careful about the English translation of *makarioi*. Every English translation of the Beatitudes makes "blessed" a predicate adjective. But this requires an implied (but missing) verb. So we get, "Blessed *are* those who." But the Greek text contains no such verb. It literally reads "Those lucky poor in spirit". The usual English translation with the added verb logically includes the idea of some sort of granted favor. This entails the idea that if I do something (like become poor in spirit), I will receive some kind of reward (like inheriting the Kingdom). The implication behind the translation "Blessed are" is that these people *have earned* something favorable. But the logical "those happy" implies no such reward. It merely describes the state of being of the subject. The adjective *makarioi* does nothing more than tell us that the subjects are lucky. It does not tell us how that luck arrived or under what conditions it exists. Until I understand the rest of the verse, I have no logical reason to *expect* anything. I am not given a guidebook for making myself lucky. The opening word simply points toward those who are *already* lucky. The Beatitude is much more like a news reporter's statement of fact than it is like a minister's prescription for spiritual gain. When I discover the insight in the second part of each Beatitude, I find that this state of bliss is not something I can earn at all. It is gift, pure and simple. But it is a gift with a very unusual twist, as we shall see.

**It's Not What You Do**

Now that we see that Yeshua is not proclaiming a right of passage for the select few (the blessed), and not announcing the results of actions taken by the

19

chosen, we are ready for the next step in his reversed logic. Who is happy? Yeshua's answer to this question is so startling, so contentious, so argumentative and so radical that the audience must have immediately taken a gasping breath in distressed unison. You see, Yeshua says that those who are jumping for joy are the ones whom the rest of society recognized as the absolutely "have-nots" – the totally bankrupt ones.

I can imagine the day that Yeshua delivered this announcement. The news of his arrival must have swept through the surrounding villages like a flash flood in a wadi.

"The prophet, the teacher, the healer – he's coming. Hurry, hurry!" Bring young Simon, the one with the open wound. Bring old Ezra who could hardly walk after the donkey kicked him. Bring Sarah, pregnant, bleeding. Bring Joshua, Jeroboam, Judas. Hurry, everyone. Be healed! Be blessed! Get something from God. God is good.

They spread out on the hill. Yeshua in the midst, touching the sick, the lame, the blind. Offering glory to the Father. And they were amazed. God was very good.

But when he opened his mouth their anticipation may have turned to shock.

It is curious that Matthew introduces the Sermon on the Mount with this odd phrase, "He opened his mouth and said . . ." This is a Hebrew idiom, reminiscent of the structure and vocabulary of the Old Testament prophets and the rabbis. It seems odd to us because it is an English translation from a Greek translation of the Hebrew, and the idiom is converted to literal word-for-word equivalence instead of

20

capturing the idiomatic expression. After all, how else does one speak unless the mouth is opened? The phrase indicates once again that the original language was Hebrew. Could it be that Matthew wanted to call attention to something special about this particular speaking - that it came not from the owner of the mouth but from the *user* of the mouth? Yeshua opened his mouth, but God did the speaking. That would have been in character with the Old Testament role of the prophet. What he spoke was equally shocking.

"Those happy poor in spirit . . ." Once again English lets us down. Our English word for poor could be the translation for two different Greek words - *ptochos* and *penes*. Both of these words in Greek carry the picture of the poor. But *penes* means the poor person who lives from day-to-day on the labor of the day. The famous images of migrant workers, the family on the porch of a run-down shack, weather worn clothes, surviving one day at a time. But nevertheless, surviving. The day laborer, without bank accounts, corporate security, health care. Eking out an existence on the fringes of our society. The *penes* - the poor. Welfare victims holding signs at the street corner, "Work for food". Yeshua gave us a few parables about these people. The most memorable one is the story about the laborers hired at different times during the day but all paid the same amount at the end of their toils.

Have you ever talked to one of these? Perhaps you have driven by and deliberately turned your head so that you were not confronted? Maybe you had a flash of shame as you felt a little humiliated by what our species has done to itself? Isn't that quick look in the other direction a silent affirmation that you, stripped of your fortunate circumstances, might be standing there too? This shame of solidarity is bad enough,

21

*but even this is not what Yeshua had in mind.* These are not the poor of Yeshua's announcement, even though they were surely in the crowd he addressed. Perhaps they were even the majority. After all, Israel was an occupied country. Work was scarce. Taxes were high. Times were hard. There were many, many *penes*.

**Beggars For God**

But Yeshua claimed that another group, the *ptochoi*, were the new millionaires. Perhaps we have better English words for these souls - the destitute, beggars, street people, homeless – the ones that are totally bankrupt. This word carries with it some very vivid pictures. It comes from a root meaning "to cower in fear or to cringe." While the *penes* of Greek society may not have been wealthy, they were nevertheless recognized as an essential part of the social structure. They were the labor force of an occupied economy, the working class, those whose personal resources, cunning and skill allowed them to get by in life, even though they had to work one day at a time in order to live. In fact, they were not so different from us. They had social status. They need not be ashamed of their economic bracket. Their distinction from the wealthy was only a relative one; they just had less. Without a credit-based economy, we might easily be just like them.

But Yeshua does not pronounce happiness on these. He speaks rather to the *ptochoi*. Their lot in life is completely different. They are **not** surviving. They are dying, right here, right now. They cannot provide for themselves, even a subsistence living. They are the homeless, the indigent, the alcoholic bums, the druggies with the shakes, the paraplegic war refuse, the masses of humanity who have been pillaged by the elite. The industrial world's legal slave labor market.  Society's catastrophes. They lead lives characterized by one thing - to be without.  They are beggars with sores on their bodies and hopelessness in their eyes.  The words used to describe them carry overtones of social disgrace.  These unfortunates had no native rights.  In great unhappiness, they were so far down the ladder of humanity that in the Greek world, they could not even invoke the protection of the gods.  In our society, they are "worthless scum".

We rarely encounter these.  Our Western world is a deliberately antiseptic one.  When I walked along Olive Street in downtown Los Angeles, I was careful not to step in the urine emanating from some cardboard box in a doorway.  When I drove along the elevated turnpike out of Newark, I looked away from the tattered figures scraping through the garbage piles.  When I crossed 10th Avenue in Manhattan, I was careful to be on the other side of the street.  Then I took a trip to Haiti and for the first time in my life, the *ptochoi* outnumbered the rest of society on a scale so immense that they were unavoidable.  Every corner of the country was crowded with the destitute, the dying, the helpless.  One of us, the incredibly wealthy Americans (by any standard in Haiti) offered three candy bars to a mother sitting on the street clutching a baby in each arm.  She refused, indicating she only wanted one.  The man persisted. She shook her head again.  Then he saw the truth. Both of the babies were dead.  If ever there was a need for luck, this was the place.  And Yeshua speaks to these – the ones whose lives are totally bankrupt.

"Jumping for joy the *ptochoi* in spirit . . ."  No one I know personally, inside or outside the circle of Christendom, is *ptochoi*.  Much has been made of the fact that in general we are the richest beings who have ever walked the earth.  Much has also been made of riches as the Christian millstone.  But

Yeshua's blessing was not for the *ptochoi*; it was for the *ptochoi* **in spirit**. It was for those whose spiritual existence emulated the characteristics of the *ptochoi*. And what kind of spiritual existence is that?

**Knees**

The overwhelming characteristic of the *ptochoi* in every age and every place is this: they know how to beg. Calluses on the knees are common to them. They were unclean, covered by the dust of the street, the grime of the garbage cans, and they knew it. It was, in fact, all that they really knew. The scraps of life. They knew that without luck they were dead. And luck came by way of abject humility. No *ptochos* could afford the luxury of defiance or the arrogance of denial. No *ptochos* could survive a single day if they allow themselves to be governed by pride. Arrogance, bravado and self-righteousness produced only one result - starvation. *Ptochoi* were saturated with humiliation. *Ptochoi* were well past the anger stage. When a disenfranchised being is angry, activity occurs. *Ptochoi* were no longer active. They were starving to death. But all of this gave them a single-minded purpose that exceeded the drive of even the greatest warrior kings. They were consumed by a goal whose clarity was emphasized with every churn of the stomach - find grace (charity) or die! Arms extended, knees bent, they cried to the passing crowds, "Alms, alms! Have mercy on us! Help us!" [7]

The "haves" of the Twenty-first Century were generally introduced to the *ptochoi* in recent years through the press coverage of Somalia, Mozambique,

---

[7] For a detailed discussion of the Hebraic background behind Yeshua's word choice, see the analysis beginning of page 138 of the Appendix.

Bosnia and other "far away" disaster scenes. That is about as close as we want to get. Just turn the channel, it's all too hideous to think about. In Yeshua's time, one only had to look as far as the edge of the road, outside of the city wall or the tombs. Nevertheless, "they" were still "over there".

In 1995, professional photojournalist Kevin Carter committed suicide at age 33. He is remembered for his Pulitzer Prize winning picture of a starving Sudanese child, huddled in the fetal position of death, while a patient vulture perched a few feet away waited for its next meal. *Time* magazine reported the suicide as a result of severe depression brought on in part by witnessing the hideous violence he photographed in his work. Carter came face-to-face with the Twenty-first Century *ptochoi* and it killed him. Most of us can remember the haunting images of starving children in Somalia. Today we view mass extermination in Rwanda, Mexico and Croatia. Our century is the most brutal in human history. We have practiced more genocide than any previous civilization. We just know how to hide it more effectively. We are sanitary, removed by the electronic filter. Face-to-face, we know that we might also seek final escape from the inhumanity of human beings.

**The Desperate Truth**

Yeshua claimed the *ptochoi* in spirit were the luckiest people alive. But I suspect that most of us are very far from such a happy event. We do not see our spiritual bankruptcy. We are not beggars for God. We are not consumed with our spiritual destitution. We do not live for crumbs from the Master's table. We do not picture ourselves huddled on the ground, surrounded by Satan's hoard, unable to offer any resistance in our spiritual headlong rush into sin and death. We can't imagine ourselves as God's homeless, living in cardboard boxes, sleeping in our own urine, eating scraps from the garbage. We are not *ptochoi* because we refuse to see the truth. We employ all kinds of defense mechanisms in order to ward off the reality that if we were confronted with our own spiritual destitution we would probably opt for the Kevin Carter solution.

Because we will not admit that we are *ptochoi*, Yeshua's announcement passes us by. We cannot receive the kingdom of heaven, God's incredible gift of unfathomable grace, because we will not beg. Our false pride means that we would rather die than admit what we really are – bankrupt without God.

I am sure that on the day Yeshua delivered His message there were many in the crowd who were offended. Poor or rich, they refused to acknowledge that they were *ptochoi*. They believed with all their hearts that self-sufficiency was the path to success. In spite of all of the hardship around them, the evidence certainly seemed to justify such a belief. Weren't the rich rich because they were hard working, aggressive, self-confident, and self-reliant? How could this teacher suggest that God's kingdom was for the *ptochoi* in spirit? Those who could not provide for themselves, who lived off of others, leeches, filthy, disgusting! There must have been murmurs, glances, knowing smiles. It was all right for a teacher of righteousness to say such things, but it would never work in the real world. So the incredible good news passed them by. They didn't have the ears to hear.

**Willing**

Yeshua asserted a fundamental theme of Hebrew Scripture when He used a word that has been translated by the Greek *ptochoi*. Yeshua connected the worthless of society and happiness. In the Septuagint, the Greek translation of the Old Testament, we find that the Hebrew word, which is often translated by *ptochoi*, comes from a root stem that means "to will", "to be willing".[8] Those who seek alms are *willing*. Willing to do what? Willing to do anything, that's what! Willing to submit themselves to utter humility. Out of complete desperation, they are willing to go to any lengths to receive. "Happy", says Yeshua, "those who are willing to bend the knee, beg, humble themselves in their plight before God". Something wonderful is coming.

Yeshua wasn't through. First he proclaimed the unbelievable congruence of the most unlikely cases - that the absolutely worthless were today's lucky winners. Those who were complete beggars before God would soon leap up in exultation. Those who did not even have enough to buy a lottery ticket won the prize. The crowd reacted.

"No, this can't be! This is just too much. What about my tithing, my attendance at every worship service, my hours of volunteer work, my special offering for the Deacon's Fund? What about the last fundraiser for the new building, the Sunday School Rally, the prayer meetings? What about all my Bible study, my orchestrated sermons, my witnessing? What about all those lost souls I've saved? Surely that counts for something. Surely God sees that I have done more than those filthy beggars. I deserve some credit, don't I?"

---

[8] Hebrew *ebyon* designates a group that is in want, needy and unable to care for themselves. For a discussion of the choice of this Hebrew word rather than the competing *dal, rash* or *anaw*, see the Appendix.

"No", says Yeshua. "There is no credit. There's only gift." And the gift is only for the ones who know they are destitute.

Then Yeshua did the impossible. He went on to say that the Kingdom of Heaven, the goal of every religious parishioner, was the exclusive benefit of these worthless examples of human spiritual existence. The translation reads, "for theirs is the kingdom of heaven." But the structure of a macarism and the impossibility of this English grammar indicate that there is a deeper meaning here.

**The Lucky Arrival**

Our question now is not, "Whom did Yeshua address as his hearers?" We know that. He proclaimed the happiness of the beggars for God. And now we have a pretty good idea what state characterizes beggars for God. The first part of the macarism is true to form; it smashes together two ideas that at first glance seem to be miles apart. The question we now must ask and answer is, "What is the relationship between the beggars for God and the kingdom of heaven?" In other words, why should those who apparently have nothing except their absolute desperation for God be so happy?

Why should they be happy? Yeshua answers, "Because those who appear to have nothing at all actually have the greatest treasure in the entire universe." This seems to be the right step. The first phrase (absolute poverty) is contradicted by the second (have it all). Certainly, there is truth here. Only those who come to God in complete agreement with His assessment of their spiritual condition (that they have nothing to offer that is worth anything at all); only those find the kingdom.

Newman and Stine suggest this is the proper understanding of the "poor". They remark that these are people who are forced "to look to God for everything, but who also receive from God the gift of the spirit (faith) to look to him for everything." [9] These poor "stand before God and recognize their absolute need for Him."[10]

They go on to say that the second part of this Beatitude has not been taken seriously by most translations. The difficulty lies in the *present tense* of the Greek. Accordingly, translators have struggled to capture the thought that the kingdom of God could actually *belong* to anyone. "For if the kingdom refers to God's rule, how can it be spoken of as "belonging to" someone?"[11] Newman and Stine call the usual translations "impossible". But the text does not allow a revision that would push the emphasis into the future or shift the focus to shared benefits.

Maybe Yeshua is saying something a little more penetrating and a little more profound.

What if Yeshua is saying that because of those who are totally destitute of their own righteousness, because of those who are complete paupers before God, the kingdom of heaven *comes* into existence? Let's try that again. The concept is a difficult one to express in English. Yeshua might just be saying that God's kingdom is a direct result of the fact that there are those who seek Him in abject spiritual poverty. The truly poor in spirit should be jumping for joy because they are the very reason that the kingdom of

---

[9] Newman, Barclay M. and Stine, Philip C, *A Handbook on The Gospel of Matthew* (United Bible Societies, New York), 1988, p. 108.
[10] *Ibid.*
[11] *Ibid.*

heaven has broken onto the scene. Their destitution, their desperation, their begging for heavenly alms causes the most fundamental shift in the entire history of everything. The Kingdom arrives.

## You're Not Getting Blessed

Let's return to the original transliteration of "blessed". If I start my interpretation of this verse with the context of "blessed", I will expect that the verse will provide some sort of entitlement or grant some sort of favor. This is what a blessing does. So I will be inclined to translate the end of the verse in the context of an expected gift – in this case, I will expect to be given the gift of the kingdom of heaven. If I begin with "blessing", I will end with some sort of view of possession. The kingdom of heaven will become an *inheritance*. Theologically, this is simply impossible. The phrase "kingdom of heaven" is completely interchangeable with "kingdom of God". It is not a place. It is a condition. It is the condition of God's reign and rule. More importantly, the phrase, "kingdom of heaven" is a euphemism for God Himself. It is the announcement of Yeshua's movement; a movement that recalls God's children to their place under the reign of the sovereign God. Yeshua is being appropriately Jewish. He does not use the divine name. Instead, He substitutes an expression that *means* the same thing as the divine name. But when this Hebrew idiom is translated into Greek, it produces a phrase that appears to be about a *place*, not a person.

Logically and theologically, no one possesses God. Even if the phrase is about God's Kingdom, we never own it. We are *participating* citizens under the reign of God. We are not shareholders. If the second part of this verse is going to make any sense, we will have to find a different understanding.

If the verse really starts with the idea of luck, then there is no expectation of earning a reward. The logic of the verse will move from a statement about *who* is lucky to the *reason* for that luck. It will not be a methodology for personal gain. So we should look at relationships, not things. Yeshua is telling us *why* these people are happy, not *what* they are going to get.

Isn't this what Yeshua said over and over when announcing the proximity of the Kingdom. "It is at hand. It is here, right now. It is dawning upon you as I speak." Isn't this what Yeshua proclaimed in His first public address. "I have come to . . ." do all those things that characterize the Kingdom's coming.[12] Only this view allows the interchangeable phrase "kingdom of God" to be substituted without strain. Only this view recognizes the Hebrew idiom and makes sense of the participation of citizens in alignment with the character of the King.

The real question is how we read the connecting word *hoti*. The Greek text reads "*Makarioi oi ptochoi to pneumati hoti*" (Happy the poor in spirit *because*). We have two choices in translating this word. The first is the common construction that views *hoti* as a preposition that introduces an independent thought. With this view, we get "because theirs is." But that makes the object of the second phrase a possession. For obvious reasons, this cannot be correct. The second choice is to use *hoti* as a connecting preposition introducing a dependent clause. This yields "because of them the kingdom of God is." Theologically, only this second interpretation rescues us from a misconstruction of the concept of the kingdom. As Schmidt clearly states, "the essential

---

[12] Compare Luke 4:16-21

31

meaning is reign rather than realm .. which comes down by divine intervention." "the being and action of God supply the necessary qualification."[13]

The kingdom of heaven is completely different than any human order. It cannot be initiated, precipitated, developed or established by any human action. It is the work of God alone. The only issue that faces Mankind is whether or not we submit to this reign as servants of the King.

And what about *ptochoi*? Are they less joyful because they do not possess something? To suggest that the kingdom of heaven belongs to them ("for theirs is") is to do travesty to the very spirit they exhibit. They know beyond any shadow of doubt that they don't own anything. They are *ptochoi* because nothing belongs to them. But, says Yeshua, they are overwhelmed with happiness, because the very fact that they recognize their spiritual destitution is exactly why the kingdom of heaven has come. They don't own the kingdom. It isn't theirs. It is God's, just like everything else. But what they do have is their poverty and that is just what is needed to usher in the riches of the Father. The gift is given to those who are bankrupt. They are the lucky ones.

**The U Turn**

This is the U turn of the first Beatitude. It is not a statement about receiving a blessing. It is a statement proclaiming the luck of those who recognize their essential desperation and the complete provision of God. The concept "kingdom of heaven" contains within it the idea that we are desperately in need. Citizens of the Kingdom are citizens precisely because they have nothing of their

---

[13] Karl Ludwig Schmidt, *basileia*, TDNT, Vol. 1, p. 584

own. They know without question that they have no part to play in the arrival of this kingdom. Its advent is the signal of God's gracious will. God's kingdom is nothing more or less than His miraculous rule arriving for me. Because I am bankrupt, I am able to receive God's arrival.

The Greek text should have given us an earlier clue. The phrase literally reads, "because of them is the kingdom of heaven." The possessive pronoun *auton* is in the first position. The emphasis of the phrase is not on the kingdom but rather on the subject referred to by this pronoun. That means the emphasis is on the *ptochoi*, not on heaven.

God's promise is as true today as it was when Yeshua uttered it. In fact, it is not so much a promise as it is a statement of fact. In God's order, in the "real" real world, only those who know that they are *ptochoi* in spirit will experience God's kingdom. The reign of grace arrives to meet their cry, simply because they have no other means, no other motive. "Sell all that you have", "Give", "Forgive", "Repent" - all of these actions are precipitated by being *ptochoi* in spirit. Those who discover the joy of the Kingdom are beggars for God. Yeshua is making a public announcement. "Shout for joy you who know that in front of God you are completely bankrupt. He heard you. And because of your begging for His grace, He is ushering in His reign". This is not a "blessing". I'm not going to get some reward. I'm being told that implicit within the recognition of my spiritual destitution is the sign that God is coming. Hallelujah! That is something to be happy about! I couldn't be luckier!

## Seductive Luck

Now the imagery of this Beatitude really strikes hard. I cannot gain God's reign and rule in my life by taking on the attributes of the poor. Even selling all that I have, sacrificing my body, giving up my life, will not bring me one step closer to the Kingdom *unless* desperation for God has overwhelmed me.

This fact should scare most of us to death. We live in a world that does everything possible to insulate us from the acceptance of our poverty. My world was made up of houses, cars, corporate paychecks, air-conditioned church sanctuaries and leisure vacations. I was light years distant from being *ptochos* economically. And that fact made it extremely difficult to remember that the truth of my existence is to be found in being *ptochos* in spirit. Yeshua said it himself. When I am wealthy, I am easily deceived. I can forget that my spiritual condition is destitution. The props of my world, all of those things on my balance sheet, act as constant delusions. Unless I get on my knees and let God examine my heart, I will never know that I am really bankrupt. Jeremiah knew my true condition (Jer. 17:9) - deceitful and desperately wicked. Only one thing can save me from myself. Begging God's grace. *Ptochos* in spirit. Find God or die! I had to lose everything for this reality to take a grip on my everyday existence. I had to become *ptochos* in this world in order to become *ptochos* for His Kingdom. And I have to go through this desperation *every day* if I am going to participate in Yeshua's movement.

The world has made an idol of self-sufficiency. We are committed to finding God in ourselves, or finding God on our terms, by which we simply mean that we will be our own gods. We amass theories, routines, disciplines, rituals - all designed to prove to ourselves that our inner resolve and inner reliance is the seat of power, fame and fortune. We flood the media with "success" images. Most of us go away in a drunken stupor. We worship the self-made person. We willingly bend our knees to this idol, as long as there is a gold embroidered cushion underneath.

Yeshua issued the declaration of our true state. Implicit in the announcement of happiness for God's beggars is the corollary that self-sufficiency or self-reliance does something terrible to us. Yeshua's story about Lazarus (whom he calls *ptochos*) and the rich man drives the message home. Riches alienate us from God. We forget our true destitution, whether our wealth is material or psychological. We become unwilling. And unwillingness makes the opposite macarism true - "Unhappy are those who are not willing" or even worse, "Unlucky are those who think they have spiritual credit because that condition means God's reign will pass them by."

Every one of us is deceived and bent toward despicable wickedness. We need sackcloth and ashes. We need groveling. We need to become *ptochoi* in spirit because we stand in the presence of a holy God. Isaiah knew it instantly. "Woe is me. I am undone for I am a man of unclean lips!"

Will you dare to take Yeshua at his word? Can you beg God for mercy and mean it? Are you willing to let God show you your real balance sheet, the real condition of your personal assets? If you're like me, you will need to overcome great resistance. The self wants no part of *ptochos*. Just bending the knees may become an incredible struggle. But God does not lie. It is *ptochoi* or *thanatos*, and *thanatos* is the Greek word for death! Yeshua makes the announcement. Only those who know they are destitute hear what He says. Only those who know they are destitute live the lucky life.

In God's lottery, you can't jump ahead and play the games out of order. If you don't win this game first, you are SOL. Desperation is the essential beginning.

**Some Desperation Questions:**

1. Have you been to the place of begging for God? Recall what it was like. How did it affect your vision of who you are? How did it re-order your priorities?

2. Do you think that you were lucky to have had that experience? Do you see God's engineering that brought you there?

3. How has your life changed as a result of your desperation?

4. Are you still completely dependent of His grace or are you slowly accumulating your own sufficiency again? Do you ask God to show you your real *daily* balance sheet?

5. Have you thanked God for your lucky desperation or are you trying to avoid being His beggar?

# $G$rieving

"Mommy, why are they all wearing black?"

She turned to the five-year-old, resolutely determined not to break down in front of him.

"It's because it's such a sad day, sweetie. They all feel so bad."

"But isn't Marie in heaven with Jesus?"

"Yes, honey. Of course she is."

"Then why are they so sad? If she's with Jesus, she's happy, isn't she?"

Five-year-olds have a different perspective on life. Maybe that's why Yeshua told us that we needed to be like little children if we wanted to really appreciate God's kingdom. We have so much trouble viewing this world as a way-station on the trip. We never have more trouble with the temporary nature of our existence than we do at a funeral. That's when we look at the second Beatitude and think, "What good is this? What difference does it make to my mourning now? I don't need comfort years from now. I need it today."

The casket was tiny, built for the little girl who lay inside. It wasn't supposed to be like this. Death snatched away this girl before she really had any life at all. Not even twelve. The tears just wouldn't stop.

Then the minister read, "Blessed are those who mourn". She wanted to scream, to jump up and tear down the pulpit. "It's not fair, God. How can I be blessed when my little girl is gone? Why? Why?" She clutched the hand of her son, shaking, sobbing. There was no relief even if Marie was with Yeshua. Sometimes just being born was bad luck.

**Luck Is Dead**

"Mourn" is a sorrowful word. We usually associate it with funerals. Someone dies and we mourn. It was the same in Yeshua's day. It is not easy to give comfort. Grief, sorrow, despair - all have a way of infecting the deepest part of our souls, turning us inward toward that place of darkness where we are most acutely aware of our loss and our helplessness. There are times in every human being's life when the utter enormity of our frail existence simply overwhelms us. In fact, it might be appropriate to say that no person finally understands the depth of the human dilemma until such an experience has been anchored in the soul. That is why the stages of life move forward and downward, from the exuberance of youth with its innocence and naivety toward the press of responsibilities in middle age to the age of memories, of death, of finality. We struggle with this journey, often caught off guard when the truth of our existence suddenly invades our usual denial and complacency. The penetration of sorrow and loss, most forcefully experienced in the death of someone close to us, reminds us that we seem too weak and too frail to command life. Reality bites – hard.

Yeshua sat with the crowd on that hillside, looking at their faces. Seeing into their hearts, he knew that each one of them swam in the stream of human grief – even if they were for the moment unaware of it. Much later, the author of Hebrews would pen the

38

final assessment of human existence – "that through death He might render powerless him who had the power of death, that is, the devil, and might free those who through fear of death were subject to slavery all their lives."[14] We're afraid, not only for ourselves but also for the power of that awful sting over those we love. Yeshua knew. From the beginning He saw His road less traveled, straight to that place in the garden when He would say, "If this cup could pass from me." It was the cup of final agony, of grief so unbearable that no human soul could live through it. He experienced the grief of carrying the judgment of separation from the One who was the real Sustainer of life.

Now, gazing over those whose lives were held in bondage by the mere fact that they were born human, Yeshua spoke His father's words. "Lucky are those who mourn, for they shall be comforted."

## Common Ground

We can imagine that the crowd grew silent. They knew mourning. They were an occupied people under harsh Roman rule. Many of them felt the lash, many had hung on the tree. And the crowds that followed Yeshua were not the noble, well fed, educated or protected. They were the poor, the lame, the beggars. They knew sorrow. Sick bodies, broken hearts. They knew grief. Starving children, anguished mothers. They knew fear. And they knew death.

Yeshua was probably more aware of this byproduct of human existence than anyone who has ever lived. He knew what it was to experience the full impact of human helplessness. Descending from the realm of

---

[14] Hebrews 2:14

the divine, taking on the form of a slave, Yeshua encountered all that human life contains to a degree that none of us will ever know. Our existence begins with our birth. We do not set aside all power and glory in order to assume the mantel of humanity. While our fall from grace is certainly real, the drop in altitude is considerably less than the chasm descent from heaven to earth. This should give us pause, not simply to consider the enormous sacrifice on our behalf, but to understand that God really *knows* how we feel. Our God is not ensconced in the lofty ethereal world, far removed from travesty, anguish and grief. Our God is the One who is intimate with human angst – "a man of sorrows, acquainted with grief". He knows us better than we know ourselves, for He is not deluded by the appearance of power, the mask of control or the promise of constancy. He knows that life is a thin red line.

There are two Greek words for "mourn". They are *threneo* and *pentheo*. *Threneo* is a technical term that indicates the ritual part of a burial when grief appropriate for the occasion is displayed. In Yeshua's time, there were professional mourners who displayed the agony of tragic death by outward signs like wailing and laments. This term captures the external, expected display associated with death and loss. This is *not* the word that translates Yeshua's announcement.

The other word for "mourn" is *pentheo*. In the Greek culture, this word falls into the category of the passions. Greeks were intellectuals. They considered passions like grief, sorrow, anger, envy and others as things to be suffered through, things that were outside of personal control, things that happened *to* you. These emotions disturbed the essential Greek balance of life. Consequently, they were to be avoided. No one could ever be happy to have these emotions rage like fire storms through the soul. Furthermore, this word is almost always associated with the grief of death. In the Greek Old Testament, it is used not only for individual sorrow at death, but also for community disaster and judgment. The message seems clear: there is nothing good about this word at all.

But Yeshua called the ones mourning "lucky"! How could they be lucky? Is it "lucky" to see your child suffer, "lucky" to know the agony of your spouse's death, "lucky" to look at a mutilated body? What could Yeshua have in mind with such an outrageous statement?

The reason that Yeshua gives for His claim that the lucky ones are those who know intimately the meaning of mourning is this: they shall be comforted. But isn't that exactly what we would expect? Don't we, even as the powerless, frail humans that we are, rush to comfort when one of our kind falls under the horror of mourning? We empathize. We sympathize. We try to comfort. That's just commonsense. So, how could Yeshua offer this as the reason for being lucky? This is just ordinary, expected response. We know that Yeshua must have had something more profound in mind to include this statement. Where is commonsense expectation turned upside down?

**Clues**

We need to pay attention to two important things from this pronouncement. First, Yeshua does not address "those who mourn". He addresses "those mourning". The verb is in the present, active sense. They are right now, at this moment, in the midst of grief. It is not past or future to them. It is the weight on the heart, the piercing blow, the gasp of breath just as the awful news hits, just as the calamity is

41

revealed. "Listen," says Yeshua, "in the center of your anguish is a promise – a promise that you are the lucky one, for something amazing is going to happen. You will be comforted."

Yes, that's true, we might say. We respond as Martha responded at the tomb of her brother. Some day God will make it all right again. I will see my brother, my child, my mother or father again – in heaven. Yes, some day. But that doesn't help much right now. Right now the pain is so deep that I can hardly breathe. Right now I am suffocating in sorrow. Where is God right now?

This is the other reason that Yeshua calls the mourning ones lucky. Those who are mourning are experiencing life at the raw edge. They are on the cusp of the spiritual/physical slice through the universe. Mourning means that they have given up their self-delusions about control, power and protection. They know that life is fragile, and that *they are not in charge.*

Most of the time we operate on the mistaken belief that life revolves around us. Most of the time we think that tomorrow will be the same as today. Only when life jolts us do we see the real picture of our existence, that we depend on God's graciousness for every breath. Mourning brings about the acute awareness of powerlessness – an essential ingredient in spiritual growth. Yeshua knew that those who were mourning were ready to receive God's gracious favor. In fact, He knew that the rest of us, the ones who still think that life is supposed to be the way that we want it to be, are far from the humility needed to find God. Those who are mourning open God's heart. He feels our anguish too. The Great Hunter-Lover reaches to us. Unless we have reached the end of ourselves, unless we are broken, like the ones who mourn, we will not notice that God is here. We will miss the great announcement: God is with us right now.

**Heaven Can Wait**

Many theologians see Matthew 5:4 as a statement about the next world. They say that this announcement is for those who mourn over the present life because they see the disaster that sin has created. They are not deluded by the appearance of this world. They know that only God's restoration in the next life will correct the horror sin has produced here. They read this Beatitude as though it is offering hope *after* death.

God will comfort us in heaven. But I don't believe that Yeshua is only telling us to hold on. We need to look harder at the backwards thinking that Yeshua wants us to see. Yeshua looked out on the brokenhearted in the crowd and saw that some were ready, poised to accept the incredible announcement about to be theirs. They were ready because they were no longer able to cope by themselves. They were the lucky ones. God could reach them, now, in the moment of their raw openness.

The rest of us were too preoccupied with our own agendas to know that God had drawn near. We loved the delusion of control and consequently, we didn't see that the Kingdom was at hand.

That brings up the second important word. The word that translates what Yeshua said about being comforted is the Greek word *parakaleo.* It is made up of two Greek words – *para* – which means "beside" and *kaleo* – the word for the action of calling. Yeshua says that those of us mourning now are lucky because we are ready to have God answer our call.

43

And it is not an answer from afar. It is the "right along side of me" response to my call. It is the comfort that comes when I feel arms around me, when I know the warmth of another's care. It is relief, right here, right now.

Yeshua knows that this comfort has two critical elements. First, it is comfort found only by those who are at this moment open because of their agony. And secondly, it is a promise that reaches beyond the immediate. The same root word for comfort in this verse is used by John to describe the role of the Holy Sprit, the Great Comforter. The Holy Spirit will come, Yeshua tells us later. He will be our "close at hand" witness, reminding us of the promises of God, and the triumph of the Messiah over the prison of death.

We no longer wait for the arrival of the Holy Spirit. Yeshua's work has been done. The Holy Spirit is a present reality in the life of every believer. This fact fulfills the promise of the Beatitude of grief. It is the guarantee that no matter what crisis comes upon us, God is here. God is in control. Our lives are not adrift on a stormy sea of emotional trauma. The Holy Spirit will stand as our Advocate when we fall. He will intercede. All of His unfathomable power, care and love will be ours because God hears our cry. There is an eschatological element in this statement that points us toward something wonderful in the future. But "They will be comforted," promises much more than relief when we enter heaven's gate. It is relief now, in this very moment. The Beatitude has a double temporal application. It says that the day will come when all the tears will be wiped away, when sorrow will cease, when heartache ends forever. God will see to it. And it says that God is seeing to it, right now. God is present to me in the very center of my mourning because God has overcome death.

In this Beatitude, Yeshua announces the most startling fact that any living person could ever hear – *death is not the end*. Death has been overcome. Could anything be more comforting? When I face the complete helplessness of my humanity, when I look into the face of death and see that everything looks like it has been lost, Yeshua tells me that *death* doesn't finish the race. God has overcome death. And God provides His guarantee of this victory by wrapping me in the arms of the Holy Spirit.

## The Paradox

Now we can see why Yeshua's announcement fits the pattern of a macarism – why it is commonsense turned backwards. We all try desperately to avoid exactly the condition necessary to experience this happiness. We all are Greeks, trying to prevent grief and loss, trying to escape the clutches of death. But until we see that this world is truly broken, that death is here and we are not in control, we will not be ready to be comforted by God. So grief comes upon us, not as a judgment or a punishment but as the single most clarifying moment of life – the moment when I see that my life is not my own, that it is not even mine to keep. At that moment, when I know my limits most intimately, I am ready to hear God's message – comfort is upon me.

But the promise is even deeper than this. From the day we are born, we begin to die. Life spirals toward death. All that we have, all that we are, all that we accomplish will be undone at the grave. Life teaches us that in the end, everything will be lost. The Teacher in Ecclesiastes seems to be right.

Yeshua stands up and says, "NO". What you thought about death is wrong. Those of you who are experiencing the terror of loss are open to God's greatest comfort. Death has been destroyed. It is not the end. Everything has not been lost. God has changed everything about our idea of death. It's not over when it's "over."

It's no accident that the word Yeshua uses here is also the word for the Holy Spirit. When Yeshua told that crowd on the hill that comfort was coming, He knew that until He died and rose again, the prison house of death held all of us in torture cells. But not now. Death is defeated. The Comforter has come.

> that He might deliver those who through fear of death were subject to slavery all their lives[15]

The grief and loss of death hold a promise. It is a promise only for those who know their true condition. It is the promise that God is still in control. It is the promise that God is able. It is the promise that God Himself will wipe away the tears. It is the promise that the jagged edge of human life is not the end.

Oh, so lucky are those who at this moment are broken over life's finality because the day is upon them when God's gracious love is at hand and they have the promise that death is defeated.

Blessed are those who mourn, for they shall be comforted.

**Some Grieving Questions:**

1. Have you experienced the terror of death?

2. What happened to you when you stood in the presence of the prison of this world?

---

[15] Hebrews 2:14

3. Did you see the fragile illusion in your thinking?

4. Did you find God's answer?

5. Are you free of the captor?

# Oppressed

## Blessed are the meek for they shall inherit the earth (Matt. 5:5)

The crucial word in the first part of the third Beatitude is the word translated "meek". Some English Bibles use the translation "gentle". Neither of these really captures the deeper meaning of this word. This is the only Beatitude that seems to be a direct quotation from an Old Testament verse – Psalm 37:11[16]. In that Psalm, David uses the word *anaw* for meek. The root word *ana* is used more than 200 times in the Old Testament. The most interesting thing about this root is that it carries the sense of being *forced* into submission or being inflicted with pain for punishment. Only through extension does it come to mean a moral and spiritual condition, denoting the inner self-inflicted pain and humiliation of contrition. Its initial sense lies in the arena of conflict, oppression and war. It is even used as a description of what God does to His enemies and the "humbling" of captured women (a euphemism for rape).

When this Hebrew word is used as an adjective, it is often connected with suffering. A person who is *anaw* is one who lives in both internal emotional affliction and external pain and suffering. This state is the opposite of what the world seeks; yet the Bible says that God uses exactly this condition to bring His people to repentance. The afflicted will rejoice when they see God's deliverance. They will find protection in His power and grace and they will follow His instructions.

---

[16] LXX Ps. 37:11 where *anaw* is translated by the Greek *praeis* leaves no doubt as to the connection.

This Hebrew background is explicitly intended in Yeshua's remark[17]. The quotation from the Psalms makes it clear that Yeshua wants His audience to recall from their history the God of the afflicted. Echoing David, Yeshua says that these afflicted ones should be jumping for joy. Consider the audience listening to Yeshua that day. These people knew what it meant to be afflicted. They were under the occupation of the Romans. The Romans had little hesitancy peppering the landscape with reminders of their supremacy. Often the roads were lined with crucified Jews who attempted to throw off the bondage of Roman oppression. We can be sure that Jewish women did not escape the desires of the conquering soldiers. The economy was in a massive depression. Tax collectors were notorious for "double-dipping". The monarchy of the Jews was nothing more than a puppet arm of the Emperor. Affliction, suffering, hardship and pain flowed freely. This isn't the kind of place you or I would want to live. Yet it is exactly the kind of place that we see in our world where war, pestilence and poverty join forces to subdue humanity. In fact, the experience of *anaw* describes the vast majority of humanity throughout history.

Yeshua tells these strugglers, "You are so lucky! You will inherit the earth".

---

[17] Some modern translations (e.g. The Jerusalem Bible) indicate that this entire Beatitude could be a *gloss*, that is, an addition inserted by someone who copied the text in the ancient past. The reasoning is that this verse is the only one that quotes an Old Testament passage and it could be seen as an extension of the first Beatitude (verse 3). But I do not believe there is any real argument for this. Once we understand the deeper meanings of verse 3 and verse 5, we see that one is not an extension of the other at all.

Let's go back to that day on the hillside.

"Did you hear what he said?" Ezra's eyes opened wider. He nudged his friend with his elbow. "I can't believe it". The crowd was electrified.

"Yeah. I heard him. He's the One for sure. He's gonna' get us out of this mess". Jacob pressed forward against the crowd. Now he was all ears. He couldn't wait for the next word from the lips of the Teacher.

Ezra wouldn't shut up. "Do you think he'll want an army? I can fight and so can my brother. You remember what the soldiers did in my village. I lost two cousins to those bastards. But now we'll show them. We're gonna' take it all back".

"Shhhh! I can't hear a thing. Shut up and listen. He just said something about seeing God".

The crowd surged to the left, carrying Ezra with it. A moment of panic swept over him as he realized that there were so many packed so close that he couldn't resist the movement. Jacob was being forced another direction. Ezra had no choice – he went with the flow. Then he became aware of the conversations around him.

"I never thought he would say it. We're going to fight back. How can we lose if he's leading us? He can feed us all, heal us too. We'll be invincible."

"I don't know. It doesn't seem right. He never talked like this before".

"Didn't he say we should be happy? What else can he mean? Look at us. We're the ones who are suffering. Now we're gonna' get revenge".

What Yeshua said must have hit home. His audience was downtrodden. They were looking for relief. And it seemed that Yeshua was offering just what they wanted. But something else was in the mind of the Teacher.

The Greek word in Matthew that we translate "meek" is *praeis* (from *praüs*). This word is not used in any of the other Gospels, a fact that is quite unusual.[18] The parallel of this teaching found in Luke 6 does not include a statement about the meek.[19] In classical Greek thinking, the word means, "gentle, pleasant, friendly, or mild". But originally the word was used for taming an animal, converting its raw, uncontrolled power into useful obedience. Applied to men, this control was seen as a virtue. The most famous example was the life of Socrates who remained calm and congenial even when he was deliberately poisoned. Serene composure in the face of abuse was considered laudable. This is another example of the Greek ideal of balance. If this is all that Yeshua meant, he would only have succeeded in reminding his audience of the power of inner tranquility. "Be happy those of you who are gentle, friendly, pleasant and mild, for some day you will have your inheritance" is hardly comfort to the abused, dispossessed and disenfranchised. It is little succor indeed to tell a woman being raped that she needs to remain calm and gentle. It doesn't go very far to remind a man being tortured that his inner life should rejoice in tranquility. Socrates was not on the

---

[18] The word is found only in Matthew 11:29, 21:5 and 1 Peter 3:4

[19] See Appendix

rack. Stoic philosophy was not a popular worldview in occupied Israel. Yeshua has more to say than this.

## It's Not Greek

Without the Old Testament background, this Beatitude crumbles into nothing more than stoicism. But with the Old Testament background, the entire concept changes. The reason that this changes everything is that unlike the Greeks, Yeshua teaches that those who are *anaw* or *praüs* experience this condition because they are within God's hand. They have succumbed to God's control. Yeshua deliberately refers to the concept in the Psalms because he wants His audience to know that affliction is not the result of an occupying army or evil men or blind catastrophe. *Affliction is a mark of God's hand on life.*

Life is a fabric of troubles. Those who suffer under it seem to be the most unfortunate ones on earth. No one in pain and agony desires such a life. But Yeshua says that precisely because God is involved in this affliction, you have reason to rejoice. You have reason to rejoice because you are actually living out some of the most important lessons of life. First, you are experiencing right now the sovereignty of God. Your world is not ruled by blind fate or irrational chaos. It is under the control and power of One who guides its movement for His purposes. You are not simply the victim of happenstance. God is at work in your life, remolding it to suit His goals. Life is a fabric of troubles because God uses trouble to shape His vessels. Is this sadistic pleasure on the part of the Great Judge? No, not at all. The history of Israel teaches that God disciplines those whom He *loves* just as earthly fathers correct and discipline their own loved children. The Bible teaches us that evil is not ultimately in charge. Your present affliction has purpose and meaning. God is working through you.

Does that mean that affliction and suffering are good? How can a God of love allow such terrible, evil acts? Yeshua makes no comment here. He simply says that life comes to us as it is. We are not in control of it. God is both the Ruler and the Judge of everything. We know that His hand covers us, whether in affliction or victory. We are asked only to submit to His will. Does that mean that we become passive toward evil? The answer is "No." God directs our lives. His permissive will for us may mean that evil befalls us. But we are also asked to stand up for Him and His holiness. That may require some very active resistance. It may even bring death, but it does not diminish God's sovereignty. What Yeshua indicates is that God can turn evil into a vehicle for His purposes. The cross will become the paradigm case of this principle. The message is clear: evil does not triumph no matter what appearances suggest.

Remember the initial meaning of the Hebrew word – to force into submission. Isn't that exactly what happens to us in affliction? We are forced to confront our oppressors and *we are forced to confront our God.* But affliction is not passive. We may not have the choice of avoiding something forced on us, whether it seems to come by accident or not. *How we respond* to this forced submission is our only choice and our true responsibility. The Old Testament context of this word means that we will see life very differently than stoic resignation to abuse. We will see that the world is God's. We will see that He is sovereign. We will see that His will prevails. We will see that affliction, suffering and pain pass through His grace before they touch our breath. We will see that submission is the hallmark of victory because it places our will under His. Finally, we will see that our response to trials and tribulations must come from His direction, not ours. Each time we submit to God's purposes in our suffering, we taste a bit of the agony in the Garden of Gethsemane and we share just a bit in what it cost to bring us redemption.

**Back to David**

To see this change in perspective, we should look at the Psalms of David. David is no timid, gentle wallflower believer. He lets his feelings show before God. He is disturbed. He is depressed. He cries out for rescue. He wants relief. Then he is shouting for joy or praising with song. But his focus is always toward God's hand on his life. Whatever befalls him, he sees it as God's confrontation. His faith is dynamic, active involvement with the purposes of God, no matter what his circumstances.

When the abused, afflicted and suffering are given a promise of relief, they face a tremendous challenge. It is the challenge of turning away from revenge, away from the balance scales of justice and toward the purposes of God. Who will rejoice in affliction? Only those who know that God's will prevails, that God is the righteous Judge who will bring peace and justice to a forsaken world. They are the only ones who can rejoice because they know that God's will is being done.

Judgment, sovereignty, purpose, power and hope are all implied in the context of "meek". These are not people who lay down without a fight. These are not spiritual wimps. These are men and women who acknowledge the Lord God Almighty as their protector, who submit to His will for their lives while battles rage in heavenly places. They are the true soldiers of the Kingdom, willing to give up their lives for their King.  God allows affliction to prepare the stage for His victory through them.

Do you see the amazing announcement here?  Yeshua tells the ones who are feeling the hand of oppression that they are very special.  They have been granted the divine privilege of suffering.  Suffering is one of God's ways of shaping us into His image and restoring His world.  It is a mark of God's love.  These people are earning the merit badge of affliction under God's special grace – the grace of fellowship in trials. This is exactly the perspective of the apostles after they were beaten by religious authorities.  They leave thanking God that they were considered *worthy enough to suffer* in His name.[20]

Do we really live with the attitude that affliction is a demonstration of God's **grace** in our lives or do we complain to God about how "unfair" life has become? Do we see our trials as God's hand shaping us into men and women who reflect His image or are we kicking and screaming our way into His presence? *Praüs* is not about mild and timid responses to life.  It is about *heroic deliberate transformation* – taking what life throws at us and turning it into a celebration of praise for God's craftsmanship through submission.  It is the power of perspective, converted and controlled.   It is the raw power of God's sovereignty domesticated in my submission, made available to His purposes.

## My Fair Share

"Incredibly lucky those afflicted for they shall *inherit*".  The next word we need to probe is *inherit*. Its Hebrew background carries the context of an "allotment" or "portion".  It is used extensively to

---

[20] Acts 5:41

describe the division of the promised land among the tribes of Israel. Behind this allotment is one central theme – divine ordination. God is the One Who promises the allotment. God is the One Who carries out this promise. The covenant is not a covenant between men and God. It is a covenant that God makes with Himself - an unbreakable promise based solely on His character. God guarantees the outcome. Nothing will prevail against it. "You who are afflicted of God, rejoice, for you shall receive your fair share". The same God who brought you into submission guarantees your allotment. There is a promise hidden in your plight. God's judgment contains His mercy. Rejoice. He has not forgotten you in your suffering. He is only preparing you for your share.

No one is more receptive to hear the words "fair share" than those who are suffering. Suffering always brings the question of fairness to the front. "Why me, God?" is the heart burden of the afflicted. Yeshua turns this question upside down. Yeshua makes us see that suffering and affliction are the *privilege* of those who are under God's rule. Suffering and affliction are the badges of our affiliation with God. Instead of the question, "Why is this happening to me, God?", we now shout an affirmation, "Let this happen to me, God!" We become the atonement for others.

On another occasion Yeshua commented on the "fair share" philosophy of life. He remarked that we should not emulate the Pharisee who stands before God and says, "Oh, God, I thank you that you have not made me like those poor beggars and those terrible afflicted ones. You made me great, wealthy, powerful". Yeshua says that people with that attitude already have their fair share. They have pandered to the world. They opted for the world's version of reward. But the man of true godly humility has a different attitude. His attitude is "Oh, God. I am not worthy. I am a sinner. Your hand on me is heavy. I can only ask for your mercy. There is nothing in me that is righteous before you". This attitude is the attitude of the oppressed. It will result in a fair share from God.

Yeshua asks us to look deeper into our suffering. Yeshua asks us to look into the very heart of the universe for our answer. That answer is to be found in acknowledging God's absolute authority over all of life, no matter what shape it takes. Submission to His will guarantees suffering. It did for the Son, it will for the Son's followers. Life is a fabric of troubles. But it also guarantees something else. It guarantees purpose and promise. God has a purpose. Submission means that my allotment is certain. God will judge me on the basis of inherited righteousness. "Thy will be done, *on earth*, as it is in heaven" means that I will receive my allotment on an earth that is under His control.

It is important to notice that the promised inheritance is not the Kingdom of God. That topic is covered in the first Beatitude. The Kingdom of God is not something that can be inherited. The allotment that we receive as the rejoicing afflicted ones is our part of the earth, not our part of God's Kingdom. In God's Kingdom we are permanent guests, not fellow owners. It is His Kingdom that we share with Him, not His Kingdom divided up among us. But the earth was created for Man and there is a sense in which we will become its true owners. Adam was given that same ownership – an ownership that carried the responsibility of being a custodian under God. God gave all that He created into the hands of Man in order that Man would manage and care for it all. That day is coming again.

Yeshua makes the most startling announcement that any of us could ever hear. Do you want to know why bad things happen? Suffering has a purpose, says Yeshua. Suffering is not accidental. Only those whom God loves enough to want to change them are given the privilege of suffering. Reverse your thinking. Suffering is homework, preparing you for your fair share responsibilities under God's command. The question "Why do I suffer?" is answered by the response "God loves me so much that He cares enough to shape who I am". The blacksmith has to heat and beat the iron to make it conform to the design he sees hidden in its structure. The sculptor has to break and hit the granite to reveal the piece of art hidden in the rock. We are works in progress. Some of God's tools are affliction and oppression.

Is life beating you up? Yeshua knew that it would. Is life unfair? Yeshua tells us to rejoice in our troubles. Why? Because His will is being done.

When God loves you so much that He puts His hand of suffering on you, jump for joy. You have a hidden promise. Grace has come to visit. You are being prepared for a special purpose.

Paul understood this Beatitude. He said "that I may know Him, and the power of His resurrection and the fellowship of his sufferings . . ." (Phil. 3:10)

The question of life has changed. It is a question that can only come from the perspective of the afflicted.

Why not me too, God?

Oh how lucky those oppressed, for God guarantees their share.

**Lucky in Suffering**

1. Are you intimately acquainted with the experience of suffering?

2. Have you recognized God's hand in your affliction?

3. Are you rejoicing in God's control?

4. Do you see how affliction has shaped your expectation of reward?

5. Can you embrace suffering as a mark of transformation?

# $H$ungry and $T$hirsty

**Blessed are they which do hunger and thirst after righteousness: for they shall be filled.  Matthew 5:6**

The fourth Beatitude is perhaps the most complex and the richest.  It is woven from fabric that has significant Old Testament threads.  Before we turn to this heritage, we need to dispel some of the common less powerful interpretations of Yeshua's pronouncement.  Once we have cleared away these misconceptions, we will be able to find the deeper meaning in his words.

First, Yeshua is not addressing a class of people made up of the hungry and thirsty.  There is no question that first century Israel was cluttered with those who fit this description.  They are referred to by a Hebrew term that means "common people", a euphemism for the poor.  The political and economic environment of Israel brought about a great mass of destitute and suffering people.  But Yeshua was not singling them out.  His statement is not aimed at those who are nutritionally suffering, either in the first century or in the twenty-first.  While this interpretation has some historical precedence, most of us will concur that Yeshua had more in mind than gathering food and drink as a result of seeking God's justice.  In other words, this is not a promise of social or political justice for the millions of poor across the world.  Of course, a byproduct of turning our lives over to God will be concern for the starving masses and attempts to meet their needs.  But this is not the focus here.

Secondly, and perhaps surprisingly, neither is Yeshua's statement aimed at those who would spiritualize this saying.   Most recent common interpretations of this Beatitude tend to follow the "spiritual" path.   We have all heard a sermon or two claiming that what Yeshua said is that we need to adopt an attitude of diligent striving for God's holy law of life, and if we do, we will find internal spiritual satisfaction.   Unfortunately, this interpretation overlooks the etymological treasures of the words used here, and as a result, leads us in the wrong direction.  Yeshua is certainly talking about spiritual issues, but I do not believe he is talking about a deep yearning for morality.  He is not telling us that those who strive after righteousness will be satisfied. Once again, the deepest motivation to see justice done will come as a byproduct of the godly life.  But Yeshua still has something else in mind.

Finally, a variation of the spiritualizing interpretation can be found even in great scholars like Bruce.  He remarks, "The hunger whose satisfaction is sure is that which contains its own satisfaction.  It is the hunger for moral good.   The passion for righteousness is righteousness in the deepest sense of the word".[21]  This makes Yeshua's statement a sort of self-fulfilling psycho-spiritual tautology (you can look up this word).  It sees the force of the Beatitude as an exhortation to adjust our perspective on life.  If we hunger for righteousness, we have already fulfilled the law of righteousness.  We are satisfied because we are already practicing the essential element of righteousness, that is, fervently desiring its application.  While this is also true - those who genuinely crave righteousness will undoubtedly bring it about because they will settle for nothing less – it is still not what Yeshua meant.

---

[21] Alexander Bruce, *The Synoptic Gospels: The Expositor's Greek Testament*, W. R. Nicoll (ed.) (Eerdmans, Grand Rapids), reprint 1990, p. 98.

Let's remember the pattern of *makarioi* (lucky or happy). Yeshua took this pattern and used it in a special way. He announced spiritual paradoxes where something considered unworthy or unacceptable becomes the pathway to reveal the hidden values of God's Kingdom. Yeshua turned the logic of the world's virtues upside-down. He forced us to think backwards. Therefore, in order to understand the real teaching of this Beatitude, we must reach back into the history of Israel.

**The History of Hunger**

The metaphor of hunger and thirst was not new to Yeshua's audience. But the imagery carried with it a great deal more than physical deprivation. In fact, the Jews remembered the passages from Deuteronomy and Isaiah where hunger and thirst were signs of *God's wrath* poured out on a disobedient people. They saw God inflict hunger and thirst on His enemies (Lam. 5:10 and Neh. 5:3) and on His chosen people (Isaiah 65:13). These people believed that hunger and thirst were signs of God's punishment and rejection. Therefore, to hunger and thirst meant to be condemned by God. This was not just a social condition. It did not demand a change in mental outlook. It could not be corrected by welfare programs or prayer meetings. It was about obedience and disobedience. It was holy judgment. My hunger was not the result of some social or political or economic circumstance. Those might be the vehicles that brought about the condition of depravity, but ultimately my hunger was the result of God's vengeance poured out on my life[22].

---

[22] The Hebrew word group comes from the root *ra'eb*, a verb that describes the condition of serious lack of nourishment. Adjectives and nouns in this group all carry the essential idea

The religious clergy of Yeshua's audience believed that God exercised control over life's physical realm as part of His moral accounting. Those who are obedient to His Law are rewarded. Those who are not obedient are punished. It is all a matter of the balance scale. If my good deeds outweigh by bad deeds, I have hope of being spared God's wrath. But if my current accounting is deficient, God may use such common human needs like food and drink to correct the scales. He may decide to punish me now, thereby rectifying the imbalance in the present, or He may withhold His immediate wrath and punish me in the future. Hunger and thirst represent two separate functions of punishment – either chastisement for the purpose of instruction and purification or suffering due to disobedience.

One other element must be added to this Jewish background. The Jewish audience was also very familiar with a *promise* connected to hunger and thirst. They knew that the prophet Isaiah foretold that God would restore Israel where none would go hungry or thirsty (Isaiah 55). In this sense, the removal of hunger and thirst is eschatological – it looks to the future vindication and reconciliation of God with hope that all of life's trials will be removed. Implicit in this promise is the idea that it is futile to seek relief from this present hunger and thirst. God has decreed it. What my present hunger and thirst should produce is an understanding that only God is the source of my sustenance. If I hunger now, my current lack of nourishment points me toward the fact that the world cannot and never will provide me with what life needs. Only God can do that. From this

---

that God is the provider of life's necessities and His hand either offers or removes these gifts. *Ra'eb* describes the chronic condition of lacking what is needed for life.

Jewish background, we now understand that even the basic necessities of life are not within our power to provide. Human beings are completely impotent even in these fundamentals. God is in control and only He can sustain us. The idea that God's verdict produces hunger as a judgment or abates hunger as a reward led the rabbinical world to a nearly fatalistic attitude toward physical calamity. If calamity befalls me, it must mean that I am unworthy. God has decreed my punishment and nothing can be done to prevent it. If God removes or restrains this calamity in my life, it must be a sign of personal worthiness before Him. We often hear a modern version of the same idea: If bad things happen to me, I must have done something bad. If I am successful and prosperous, I must have done something good. Don't we say, "What goes around, comes around" and "They got what they deserved". We could call this belief the *Law of Just Rewards*. This is exactly the concept that Yeshua overturns.

## Greek Distinctions

Now let's turn to the Greek background. There are two Greek words for hunger, *limos* and *peinao*. *Limos* is hunger in the extreme, closely related to famine. It carries the sense of a *fatal* need. *Peinao*, on the other hand, means a chronic lack of nourishment. The difference between these two Greek words is the difference between starvation and chronic malnutrition. Notice that both of these words refer to a *lack* of sustenance, not a striving for sustenance. This is an important element for understanding the deeper meaning of Yeshua's statement. Two things become clear from the Greek. First, the Beatitude uses *peinao*, not *limos*. We are talking about a chronic state of deficiency, not a catastrophic fatal situation. Secondly, the sense of this word points us toward those who are being deprived of something essential to life. Therefore, Yeshua is talking to those who are the *passive* victims of this situation. These people have experienced circumstances that have taken from them something absolutely essential for living. They are not fervently striving for righteousness. Rather, what they need for survival is missing from their lives and they are now dying without it.

Goppelt summarizes this eloquently:

> The hungry are men who both outwardly and inwardly are painfully deficient in the things essential to life as God meant it to be, and who, since they cannot help themselves, turn to God on the basis of His promise.[23]

Who are these people that Yeshua calls "Lucky" (Blessed)? They are not some group of people we can point to. Their old clothes, their empty wallets, their homeless shelters or even the lack of food on their tables does not identify them. They are the people who are singled out by their own internal, keen awareness of the need for something essential. They are the ones who know that life is missing something vital, something that can only be supplied by God Himself. They are the ones who recognize that the elements needed to make life what God intended life to be are painfully absent. They know something very important. They know that *they cannot provide whatever it is*. They are helpless to rectify this situation.

Think of this example: You are a miner trapped far underground by a massive cave-in. You know that people are on their way to rescue you, but right now, at this moment, your most vital need is oxygen. It is running out and as your breathing gets harder and

---

[23] Goppelt, "πειναω ( λιμο )", TDNT, Vol. 6, p. 18

harder, you know that there is nothing you can do to provide yourself with this critical element for life. No matter how hard you try to conserve, every breath brings you closer to dying, but you cannot stop breathing. Your lack of oxygen becomes the most important fact of your life. Yeshua is speaking to those who realize that their lack of righteousness is the most important fact of their lives. Without it, they will surely die. Something that they must have is lacking and they have no ability to provide it for themselves.

Remember the Law of Just Rewards. Yeshua shocked his audience by telling them that precisely those people who appeared to be under the judgment of God are really in a state of pure luck. Everyone supposed that if you were suffering from chronic malnutrition it was a sign that you were being punished for your unworthiness. Everyone supposed that if you were well fed and wealthy it was a sign that you were upright and worthy. Yeshua turned all of this upside down by saying that those people who were *chronically helpless* in their need for worthiness are lucky. Their need was going to be taken care of.

"O, how lucky those of you who know that you cannot provide what you need by yourselves, who know that life is not giving you what you must have, who know that you are dying without what only God can provide. JUMP FOR JOY! Your day has arrived."

Everything about Yeshua's proclamation was wrong, according to the legalists' view of religion. God could never count as worthy those who were essentially unworthy. Don't we say the same thing today – "God helps those who help themselves". Every effort to earn God's blessing, every bit of striving to make myself into something acceptable to God – all of it –

Yeshua casts aside. God is for those who know they don't have a prayer.

What essential element of life do these people lack? It is not bread. It is not water. It is God's righteousness.

The Greek word for righteousness is *dikaiosyne*. It comes from a Greek root that means "justice". The concept of righteousness is closely linked to the Hebrew concept of Torah. God's law (His Torah *instruction*) was the most powerful expression of His covenant with His chosen people. The Torah is not just the legal proclamations of the Ten Commandants or the laws given in Deuteronomy and Leviticus. The Torah is God's rule governing all aspects of life found in the stories, the history, the poetry and the legislation of the first five books of the Tanakh (the Hebrew Scriptures). The Old Testament consistently affirms that God's rule is the proper order for all life. This concept is very different from our modern Greek based legal system. The Greeks believed that Law was essentially a result of rational implementation of what benefited the state. Law was what is proper and what is established for the good of the citizenry. This concept is not present in the Hebrew view of Torah. The Hebrew view of Torah begins and ends with God. Unlike the Greek concept of Law, God is not subject to some higher principle that He merely administers in the world. God Himself is the embodiment of righteousness. The Torah is simply an expression of His character as the Holy God. God is *The* Ruler Who establishes the conduct code of His kingdom based on what He knows to be true because it is the expression of His very Being. Because He is The Ruler of all that is, He is the proper authority for the expression of any principle governing life. His instructions are unchangeable and incontestable. God is the interrogator, prosecutor, judge and jury concerning conformity to this code of conduct. Righteousness is the term used to express the idea that God is both the Lawgiver and Judge.

Nevertheless, God's righteousness is not a static set of rules to which human beings must ascribe. God is actively engaged in the exercise and application of His righteousness. God's instructions for living are not like the Greek idea of conformity to what is proper. God's rule is the active involvement of His righteousness with our deficiency. In simple terms, God is holy. We are not holy and can never be holy based on our own efforts. We will forever fall short of God's standard. But this does not mean that God casts us aside as unworthy. Amazingly, in spite of our unworthiness under His own instructions for life's order, He counts as righteous those who recognize their unrighteousness and seek His help. We can think of the stories of Abraham, Moses, David, Isaiah, Daniel and many others who knew their essential unworthiness in front of a holy God and yet, God established them as righteous.

In the days of Yeshua, some of the rabbinical clergy believed that right standing in front of God (righteousness) was based on godly behavior. In other words, they thought that if they kept all the rules, their human efforts would result in a balance in their favor and God would reward them. For this reason, some scribes and Pharisees[24] were meticulous about rule keeping. This was incredibly serious business. Their lives hung in the balance, both in this world and the next. Yeshua attacked this

---

[24] I want to be very clear that this religious view does not apply to *all* the scribes and Pharisees. Rabbinic material clearly demonstrates that many of these men held the same views as Yeshua. To categorize them all as enemies of Yeshua is a serious "Christian" error.

belief and practice over and over as nothing more than self-righteous sinfulness. No wonder these members of the religious establishment were so opposed to Yeshua. Yeshua proclaimed that no man could earn his way to God – a statement that challenged everything about the purpose of this rule-keeping religion. This is the same argument we find in Paul's letter to the Galatians. It's not about an essential tension between "law and grace." It's about the confusion of the purpose of "law" (Torah instructions) and grace. Grace saves! "Law" provides life direction so that our behavior will serve His purposes. The authors of the New Testament material, and the majority of rabbinic teaching did not suggest that a man can *earn* his way into God's favor. They all knew that was impossible. That's why there are *sacrifices*. Grace is God's gift. It has always been God's gift, but it does not erase the need for God's instructions about how to live *after* one has received the gift. The real theological battle was the difference between this view of grace-Torah and the view of the legalist who claimed one must *first* keep the "law" before grace could arrive. Furthermore, Yeshua claimed that no man could find favor with God except through him. From the perspective of legalism, this was insanity, megalomania and blasphemy.

On the hillside, Yeshua speaks about right-standing before God. The first thing that he says is that his message is only for those who already know their essential depravity. They feel the pangs of unworthiness, the dregs of life out-of-synch, the pain of knowing that life was not intended to be like this. And they also know that they can't do anything about it. They are helpless victims of the lack of righteousness. They need something that they cannot give themselves. They need to be right with

God but they know that nothing they can do will make it happen.

Yeshua amplified this Beatitude in a parable. His story helps us to see the bigger picture. A son who believed that he had a right to his own life left home with his inheritance. When his fortune was gone, he realized that what he needed in order to survive was the provision from his father's house. So he returned to beg only for the sustenance given to a servant. He came in complete humility, devastated by his own unworthiness, begging no more than enough to survive. But the father was so overjoyed at his return that he showered his son with everything needed for a full life and more. The son's intimate knowledge of his unworthiness became the ground of his acceptance.

It is important to know that the literal translation of this Beatitude is "Lucky those hungering and thirsting". This is a *present tense* experience. This promise is not for those who experienced something in the past. It is not for those who may come to this place in the future. It is for those who are right now, at this very moment, aware of their desperate need. It is present tense, immediate, desperation. Just like the first Beatitude, these people are keenly aware of the fact that if something doesn't change their condition; they are going to starve to death.

Yeshua says to them, "Rejoice! You are going to be filled". The last word we need to examine is this one – "filled." "Filled" isn't quite right. This word is a form of *chortazo* and it comes from the Greek word that means "grass". It means "to be fed". Oh, the depth of God's word. How marvelous it all is! Yeshua tells those who know they cannot bring about their own righteousness, "It be provided for you." They are going to be fed. They do not need to forage in

70

life's garbage piles to find enough to sustain themselves. They don't need to build up some spiritual bank account of goodness. God is going to provide them with exactly what they are missing. There is a rich heritage that supports this teaching. Consider the following Old Testament passages:

Ps. 23: 2  He makes me lie down in green pastures.
Ps 79:13  Then we thy people, the flock of thy pasture.
Ps 100:3  we are his people, and the sheep of his pasture.
Jer 50:19  I will restore Israel to his pasture
Ezek 34:14  I will feed them with good pasture
Ezek 34:31  And you are my sheep, the sheep of my pasture, and I am your God
Zeph 3:13  For they shall pasture and lie down,
1Sam 2:5  but those who were hungry have ceased to hunger.
Neh 9:15  Thou didst give them bread from heaven for their hunger and bring forth
Isa 49:10  they shall not hunger or thirst,

But Yeshua is not finished. He is not a prophet pointing to some future restoration of righteousness by God. He knows that those who live with the agony of their insufficiency before God need help now. Yeshua is announcing something incredible. He is proclaiming that God's solution to this yearning is being disclosed *right now*. He said "I am the bread of life; he who comes to me shall not hunger, and he who believes in me shall never thirst" (John 6:35). He said, "I am the door. If anyone enters through me, he will be saved and will go in and will go out and will find pasture" (John 19:9) and "I am the Good Shepherd" (John 10:11). Yeshua is the answer to the problem of hungering and thirsting for righteousness.

Let's attempt a fuller translation. "Rejoice and jump for joy you who at this very moment know that your helpless lack of worth before God is killing you. You are incredibly lucky. I have come to restore your righteousness before God."

Yeshua is declaring happiness to those who know their lives are inadequate. Do you know what it is like to be constantly inadequate in your standing before God? Has your life been under the specter of slow death from the lack of His grace? Can you feel those racking pains that accompany spiritual starvation? If you answer, "Yes", then you are most fortunate. This is not judgment. It is grace. This Beatitude is not about your efforts to bring righteousness into the world. It is not about your striving for the application of God's rule. It is not about the desire for morality or a program of spiritual purification. It is about your total and utter inability to fill your most basic need of life – to be rightly related to our Creator. It is about that moment in your life when you know that how you live and what you live for is all wrong, and you just can't fix it. It is about the instant when you realize that you are completely helpless in your efforts to find righteousness for yourself. All you can do is cast yourself on God. Rejoice, says Yeshua. I am the way, the truth and the life. I have found you. And I will fill your desperate need.

Yeshua's macarism is a thought-provoking saying that reverses ordinary understanding by providing a new and deeper way of looking at the same thing. It stands commonsense on its head. Yeshua points to the basic necessities of life as a symbol of another basic essential – righteousness. But what Yeshua says to each of us is that we are helpless when it comes to all life's necessities, including this one. Only God can provide them, even if we fail to acknowledge

His blessing.  And those who will receive the most precious of all essentials, righteousness, are the ones who are most keenly aware of their complete inability to provide for themselves.  When we are finally starving for God, He arrives.  It will not happen while we try our own versions of ethical purity.  It will not happen while we measure our deeds by balance-scale goodness.  The only ones who are going to be blessed in this macarism are the ones who have nothing to show for themselves except their need.

In our modern world, it is very important to see that Yeshua does not say that we are lucky because we *will be empowered*.  He doesn't promise a sudden insight or spiritual trick that will make us acceptable or even capable of getting what we need.  **The desire for righteousness is not self-fulfilling**.  What Yeshua says is that righteousness will be "fed" to you.  We are not going to suddenly be empowered to belly-up to God's table and eat our share of righteousness.  No, we can only receive righteousness when we are so malnourished in ourselves that we require God to spoon feed us.  The secret of receiving righteousness from God is to come to God without any self-ability at all.  It is no different than feeding the starving children in Somalia.  Carried in on stretchers, unable to do anything for themselves, hovering near death unless they receive a blessing from someone else's storehouse, we watch the doctor or nurse feed them one spoonful at a time.  In the same way, God will feed us what we must have in order to live, one spoonful at a time.  But only when we reach the absolute end of our own self-rights.

In an age when personal rights are in the forefront, we as Christians would be well served by taking this Beatitude to heart.  There is no personal bill of rights for a Christian.  There is only unmerited, undeserved grace from the Creator God though His Son Yeshua

73

the Messiah. Standing on my personal rights automatically excludes me from those who hunger and thirst. Claiming personal merit means that I focus on my self-rights rather than on rightful selflessness. When my rights become the standard of life, I exclude myself from being fed by the grace of God. I remove myself from those who are characterized by a lack of life's essentials. The result is that I cannot receive God's bounty. It's a world turned upside-down. God gives to those who cannot offer anything except their need. Blessing falls on the undeserving. Only those with hungry eyes will see it.

> They shall hunger no more, neither thirst any
> more; . . . for the Lamb which is in the midst of
> the throne shall feed them, and shall lead
> them unto living fountains of waters; and God
> shall wipe away all tears from their eyes.
> (Rev 7:16-17)

## Lucky Insufficiency

1. How has your true insufficiency been revealed to you?

2. Where does God meet your needs?

3. Do you trust Him to completely provide?

4. Are you willing to be fed?

# $\mathcal{L}$osers

**Blessed are the merciful for they shall receive mercy.   Matthew 5:7**

"You get what you give." Doesn't this Beatitude seem to tell us what is obvious? If we show mercy to others, God will show mercy to us. Pretty simple. So simple that Robinson calls it "a self-acting law of the moral world". But if it's just commonsense, why did Yeshua say it? We're missing something here.

Sometimes Christian concepts have had such powerful influence on our ordinary culture that we become immune to their radical nature. This is one of those times. We will discover the power of Yeshua's teaching here only if we unhook the moral and ethical influence that has been part of our western Christian upbringing.

In this verse, we have the familiar opening pattern. *Makarioi* – Lucky! Joyful! Yeshua is making an announcement. This is not a conditional command. It is *not* a statement that says "You should be merciful so that you will get mercy". This is not a variation of the Golden Rule. Yeshua is announcing that those who *are already practicing mercy* are lucky. Literally, the phrase reads "Lucky those merciful". Yeshua is proclaiming a statement of fact, not an invitation to action.

Our English word "mercy" is a word taken from the legal context. We imagine a courtroom scene. The guilty person stands before a judge waiting to be sentenced. He falls to his knees and begs for mercy. He is asking that the sentence he deserves be set

75

aside.  For us, mercy is about removing punishment. But it didn't always have this kind of meaning.

## Greek and Jews

The Greek word is *eleemones* from *eleos* (compassion, mercy, pity).  It is used twice in this verse.  The word is very old.  In the Greek culture it was considered one of the passions (from *pathos*).  For the Greeks, passions have a very special classification.  They are *emotions that come over us.*  We don't control them. They control us.  We are the *passive* recipients of these disturbing and upsetting fluctuations of the soul.  Grief, envy, lust, sorrow, mercy, joy, rage or fear – whether good or bad – we are the victims of these tidal waves of feelings.  Greek philosophers believed that a life battered by emotions was a life out of control.     They sought a balanced, uniform, *unemotional* life – a life in the middle, calm and free from the disturbances of life's uncontrollable turmoil. Aristotle tells us that we are better off *without* these emotions.

In the Greek culture, mercy was not a moral or legal consideration.   It was a psychological emotional response.  We are swept into the emotion of mercy when we come into contact with someone who is experiencing *undeserved* suffering.  Something in us responds to the plight of another.  We just can't help it.   And this creates another problem in the Greek mind.  Mercy is connected with *fear*, the fear that what has happened to this person who has aroused my feelings of mercy might also happen to me.  Mercy is not a passion that is aroused when we see someone suffering because they deserved it.  We don't feel sorry for them.  Actions have consequences.  If they are suffering because of justified consequences, then that is right and just.  No mercy is required.  It is *undeserved* suffering that births mercy in our souls.

And precisely because it is undeserved, we fear it. Since there is no apparent reason for this tragedy, it also could happen to us.

Mercy does play a part in the Greek idea of justice, but not because justice requires mercy. If fact, just the opposite is true. Justice requires punishment. The only escape from what we deserve when we have broken the law is mercy. We must plead for mercy instead of punishment if we are to be freed from the inevitable consequences of our crimes. But the Greeks believed that the proper response to those who deserved punishment was wrath. Mercy was not expected in judicial decisions. In fact, mercy was *a sign of weakness* for it diminished the law. The merciful judge was one who could be swayed and was therefore not dependable. He just might overturn the just requirements of the law. Real judges kept their hearts *out of the picture*.

In the final stages of Greek philosophy, the Stoics argued that mercy was "a sickness of the soul" and was an unworthy emotion for those who were enlightened. This seems entirely uncaring to us today, but remember that mercy was considered an overpowering and uncontrollable emotional response. It did not have moral consequences. It only made life more upsetting. The Greek ideal was a life like Mr. Spock on *Star Trek*. As a Vulcan, Spock was not subject to human emotions like Captain Kirk. His life was completely controlled by reason.

All of this changed when the Old Testament was translated into Greek. The Hebrew word that was translated by the Greek *eleos* (mercy) is _hesed_. This word occurs more than 400 times in the Old Testament. Esser, in the *Dictionary of New Testament Theology*, tells us that the Hebrew concepts behind this word "betray a completely different background of thought from the predominately psychological one in Greek".

In the Old Testament, mercy is part of the covenant relationship. It is an obligation between parties in the covenant. The stronger party shows mercy to the weaker party. Mercy means the act of giving help to one who is in need. In the Old Testament, mercy is tied directly to knowing God (Hosea 6:6). This Hebrew word (*hesed*) has quite a controversy about its full meaning. It seems to be related to the bond between God and His people. Yet it does not mean that God shows kindness toward His people simply because they have a covenant with Him. Rather, it indicates that behind God's promises to any of His children lies God's love for His own creation. God loved us before He made promises to us. In fact, His help toward us was not dependent on our keeping the terms of the relationship outlined in the Law. No one has done that. Jews do not believe they *earn* God's favor by being obedient to the Law. That idea is a mistaken Christian interpretation. Obedience comes from gratitude, not employment. God desired to rain His love and compassion on us when we need it most, *before* we have a good relationship with Him.

It is important to understand the difference between grace and mercy. Grace is about God's free gift of redemption and His forgiveness of our active rebellion against Him. Mercy is God's alleviation of the *consequences* of sin. It is the repair work that God performs to overcome the destruction that our sin has caused. Mercy follows grace. When God grants mercy to us, it is a pardon to the undeserving. But unlike the Greek view, when the Judge of all Mankind grants mercy by removing the consequences of sin, it is never viewed as partiality or a sign of weakness. It is viewed as a sign of the covenant promise – the stronger party coming to the rescue of the weaker.

Because mercy is part of the fabric of the covenant, it is not a deficiency. In fact, mercy demonstrates God's strength. He is so powerful that He is able to release us from punishment without compromising the Law. How He does this is the story of the crucifixion.

The New Testament is written in Greek, but it is not Greek in its thinking. By examining the background of the word for mercy, we discover that the Greeks thought of mercy as a detriment to the soul, something to be avoided. It caused life to spin out of control and it brought on fear. The Greek ideal was structure, order and rational control not buffeted by the storm of unruly emotions. Mercy was about emotions in opposition to the regimentation of the Law. To grant mercy was to diminish law and justice. For the Greeks, society depended on correct behavior. So, correct behavior was rewarded and incorrect behavior was punished. Anyone who fell prey to mercy was likely to lessen the bond between behavior and consequences. Therefore, mercy was a weakness that interfered with the strength of will. Like all emotions, mercy was not under the control of reason. Since the Greeks viewed reason as the final criterion of Man, uncontrolled emotions belonged to a world they wished to leave behind.

The Hebrews had a completely different picture. Mercy was all about morality, not about emotions. Mercy was the blessing of God in spite of the demands of the Law. It was a sign of God's loving kindness toward His people. Mercy made life possible because without it everyone would be punished. Unlike the Greeks, mercy was the purest act of will because God Himself made the choice to set aside deserved punishment. Mercy is not an overpowering emotion that robs the will of its power. Quite the opposite. Mercy is the supreme example of God's will turning away justifiable wrath. In this

79

view, mercy was completely within the control of reason. In fact, showing mercy was the *logical* thing to do. It was built in to the idea of the covenant, a final expression of God's supremely reasonable control.

These differences might cause us to ask some penetrating personal questions. What motivates mercy in your life? Are you Greek? Do you run from the powerful emotions of compassion in order to maintain a nicely balanced existence? Or are you Hebrew, embracing amelioration of punishment for those who *deserve* it because you want to reflect the character of God? You can't have it both ways.

**Clash of the Titans**

These backgrounds clash in this Beatitude. But both backgrounds have something to say to us.

Yeshua says, "Lucky those merciful". If we think about this for more than one spiritualized moment, we will see that this thought is already backwards. First we must notice that Yeshua is not addressing the ones who *need* mercy. He is addressing the one who *gives* mercy. He is talking to the ones who are on the right side of justice. The law tells them that they *rightfully deserve reward*. The Law is in their favor.

We usually read this Beatitude as though it is speaking to the transgressors, the ones who deserve to be punished. That mistake makes us think that the opening announcement of this Beatitude proclaims mercy to the ones who are guilty under the Law. But look again! Yeshua is addressing those who *are at this moment giving mercy*. These are not the guilty ones. The guilty have no right to *give* mercy. The people that Yeshua has in mind are the ones who have been the *victims* of crimes. They are the ones who deserve justice. The law is in their favor. I can only give mercy if I am worthy of justice. I must be the *offended* party if I am going to grant release from punishment for someone else.

This makes the Beatitude's announcement much more startling. Why should the merciful be lucky? They are precisely the ones who are **not** getting their rights. People who show mercy have put aside their just reward. Yes, it's true that the ones who receive mercy should be grateful (they aren't always though, are they?). But the very fact that I give mercy means that what should rightfully happen to me is not going to happen. *I deserve justice. But I let it go.*

Now we begin to see how much we are really Greek in our thinking. Imagine this picture. We attend a trial. The plaintiff (victim) has been severely injured, slandered and defrauded. The case is open and shut. Damages are determined and punishment allocated. But then the victim stands and says, "Your Honor, I know that this man is guilty. The court has confirmed his guilt. But I would like all the damages waived and the punishment removed. I want to let it all go. In fact, *I want to take all the consequences on myself.*" How would we react?

"You can't be serious. You just won. It's rightfully yours." That's the lawyer talking.

"How can you do this? After all we've suffered, how can you just let him go?" That's the spouse.

"You must be out of your mind. All that money and you'd be set for life. You're crazy." That's the friend.

"What a loser! This guy is so stupid he doesn't deserve to win." That's the news reporter.

It's all the same Greek thinking, isn't it? Justice must be served. Consequences are demanded. You won, now you collect.

"Lucky those demonstrating mercy". Someone in middle-Eastern garb in the back of the room is clapping.

**Giving It Up**

Many years ago my brother came to me in great need. He was suffering and desperate. He needed money, immediately. It's true that the circumstances that brought about his need were of his own making, but I could sympathize. I have been in awful circumstances too. So, I loaned him what he asked for. "I'll pay you back as soon as I get my next paycheck". I showed sympathy but I had not yet experienced mercy. Mercy only became a reality for me when I wrote to him years later telling him that I was wrong to act as though the money God had entrusted to me was mine to distribute. It was not mine. It was God's. And God believes in active compassion.

The money has never been returned. Yeshua said to me, "You have a choice here. You can be unhappy that you were sympathetic. You can feel abused and used. You can tell yourself that you deserved justice. Or, you can listen to what I am announcing. You can show real mercy. You can let it go. You can forgo justice. You can accept the loss as your own. If you do, I pronounce you Lucky!"

I wrote that letter. I told my estranged brother that it was not my place to decide how God wanted to use the money He had generously given to me. I was wrong to put conditions on his need. I asked him to forgive my selfishness and not to repay the debt.

What justice demanded was set aside because I understood how mercy had affected me.

## The Cost

When mercy becomes personal, it is not about sympathetic affiliation. It is not about emotional compassion and identification. It is about *giving up my right to justice*. Only those who deserve justice can show mercy because mercy means that the rightful consequence of justice is no longer applied. You can sympathize, empathize, identify, show compassion, understand, care or be supportive without being merciful. In order to show mercy you must have something at stake. You must make a sacrifice. **It has to cost you something.** Mercy is giving up what's mine – not because the other person deserves a break, but because I realize that mercy is valuable by itself. What I discover is that mercy produces personal psychological freedom. I place my right to justice in the hands of God. It is no longer a weight that I carry. I am free. God can do what He wishes with the situation. It's no longer mine.

Yeshua knew that mercy was about sacrifice. It is about the sacrifice of making choices. You see, the Greeks were wrong. The emotion of mercy, the overwhelming disturbance of soul that comes when we are confronted with one like us who is tormented, is not something to be avoided. Life is intended to bring us face to face with sorrow and grief. There is a reason for this: God wants us to see our real status in His court. But the Greeks did not have a personal Creator and Judge behind their philosophy. They only had Law (with a capital L). So, mercy made them afraid. Mercy confronted them with life as uncontrollable reality – the truth as it really is. And without God, there is only fear.

Mercy is the summary word of the life of Yeshua. He made a choice that cost. He gave up being God to be like God's enemies – one of us. And mercy cost God too. He lost His only son to the sacrifice for those who deserved to die. Punishing Yeshua for our sins cost God the Father the unfathomable sorrow of losing someone He loved forever. A person who didn't deserve any of it. To show mercy is always expensive.

But Yeshua tells us something wonderful. Those who are merciful are overwhelmed with another emotion – joy. "Lucky", he says, because they have reflected true reality. They know there is a price for mercy. And they have decided to pay it.

Now we must ask the question that haunts this Beatitude. Do we show mercy *in order to* receive mercy? What is our motivation for being merciful? The answer is found in the relationship between the conjunctive ("because") and the second phrase ("they shall receive mercy").

**Connections**

The Greek word *hoti* connects the two phrases. We usually translate it as "because". So, we read, "Lucky those demonstrating mercy **because** they will receive mercy". If I read the Beatitude with "because" in the translation, then I might conclude that the reason for the happiness Yeshua announces is due to the fact that these people will receive like-kind action, that is, they will be rewarded for their mercy with mercy. Therefore, they are happy because they know that they are going to get what they have given up. Where they willingly turned down what they deserved, someone else will in turn let them off the hook. They simply paid the price of a future annulment today. They collect relief for themselves tomorrow. This makes the Beatitude a self-fulfilling moral law. But if this is a *macarism*, *hoti* cannot be understood in this way.

Fortunately, there is another reading. *Hoti* after words of emotion such as joy, pity, sorrow or rejoicing (happy) can be translated "seeing that". The translation change from "because" to "seeing that" is subtle and requires careful analysis. First, we must clear away the false conception that Yeshua is addressing guilty people. When Yeshua says, "Lucky those merciful ones" he is talking to the people who stand in the role of the *judge*, not the criminal. Secondly, we need to be careful not to allow our previous conceptions about "blessed" to interfere with the correct understanding. This is not a statement of bestowing favor. It is not a blessing. It is an announcement of a present experience without any connotation that there is some future expectation of reward. When Yeshua says, "Lucky those merciful ones" he tells us that they are lucky simply because they are merciful, not because they expect to be shown mercy. This distinction is crucial but difficult to capture because we are so used to reading this Beatitude from the perspective of the criminal. We think, "Yes, I am guilty so if I show mercy, then I will get mercy." But this is not the perspective of the Beatitude. The Beatitude takes its perspective from the eyes of the justified man – the one who does not need mercy because he is in the right.

Recall the Greek background. Showing mercy in a Greek court was a sign of weakness. It made the merciful person suspect because it demonstrated that such a person could be swayed by considerations other than the demands of the Law. Furthermore, the Greeks sought balance by avoiding mercy. Mercy led to fear and worry.

85

But Yeshua counters this entire premise by saying that the "weakness" of mercy is the avenue to happiness. Mercy leads to peace and calm. In order to make this claim, Yeshua offers a theological ground for mercy. This is not a reward. It is the *raison d'être*, the underpinning reason.

Mercy leads to happiness (seeing that) the offering of mercy is the requirement of my own need. Yeshua says, "Lucky those paying the price of being merciful. They understand why mercy will be shown to them". This change is essential to the structure of a macarism. You see, I don't show mercy *in order to be rewarded* with mercy. I show mercy *as a result of knowing why* mercy is essential for me. It is the fact that I am a candidate for mercy that makes me willing to pay the price of mercy now. It is not my *reward*; it is my **obligation**.

Who can show mercy except those who know that they deserved wrath but were spared? Mercy is not a natural human emotion or a necessary human act. That is why the Greeks feared mercy. It was unnatural. It took you out of place. It disturbed your commonsense balance by upsetting the delusion of control and the illusion of fairness. Mercy is expensive, so expensive that we would rather not consider it. It reminds us of how desperate we really are.

Yeshua turns all of this upside down. Mercy must be an act of the will precisely because it is a denial of the self. It declares amnesty for those who have harmed us. It makes us pay for their sins. And it is only possible because God shows us what it means to pay the price before we ever consider the possibility.

*Hoti* tells us that we are essentially the same as the one standing guilty before us. He deserves punishment. So do we. "Seeing that" we know our own unworthiness, we must show mercy to the unworthy. This Beatitude is God's confirmation that our essential unworthiness has been acknowledged and annulled. We, who deserved the reward of justice, set aside that reward because we know that we also deserve the punishment demanded by justice.

This interpretation is confirmed by the verb in the second phrase, "thcy shall receive mercy". The verb is future tense passive voice. It is not something that we can do for ourselves. We are the *passive recipients* of this future act of mercy. That means it cannot be bestowed on us as a reward since rewards are *earned* by the *active* efforts of the recipient. If showing mercy entailed earning mercy, this Beatitude would be a self-fulfilling moral law. But showing mercy does not entail earning mercy. There is no *necessary connection* between the happiness of being merciful and the future annulment of my deserved punishment. Mercy cannot be earned. It must be given by a stronger, justified party to a weaker, unjustified party. Therefore, this Beatitude cannot be a Law. It is the expression of God's *unnecessary* benevolence. That's what makes it so wonderful! No wonder we shout for joy. God has confirmed that we, the ones showing mercy, will find He is merciful too.

"Oh so lucky you merciful ones seeing that you now know God is also merciful".

## Lucky Losers

1.  Have you ever shown real mercy, mercy that came with a price, to someone?

2.  What did it feel like?

3.  Did your experience help you realize that you also needed mercy?

4.  Have you experienced the mercy you did *not* deserve?

# $D$irty

**"Blessed are the pure in heart for they shall see God" Matthew 5:8**

We have an English word that is the direct descendent of the Greek word used in this Beatitude. But it isn't "pure". The Greek word that is translated "pure" in this verse is *katharos*. Our direct descendent in English is "catharsis". In both Greek and English, the meaning is really "purged" or "cleansed". It's easy to see how it could be translated "pure" since that is the result of being cleansed or purged, but there is just the slightest shift in meaning. That shift makes a difference. If the word is "pure", we immediately think of something that requires no further improvement. It is perfect in itself. But "cleansed" immediately implies that it was once not acceptable and has now been altered. The emphasis is on the process that brings about this condition called "cleansed." The Beatitude asks us to examine those who enjoy the bliss of having been cleansed. The natural question is, "How did this happen?"

Let's examine the background of this word *katharos*. There are two Greek words that are translated "pure". One is *katharos*, the other is *hagnos*. The background of *katharos* is ritual cleansing. The background of *hagnos* is holiness (it comes from a word meaning "to stand in awe"). It is immediately apparent that Yeshua deliberately talks about purity in the sense of religious ritual, not about purity in the sense of moral holiness before God. Why would he do this?

One of the consistent messages of Yeshua was the need of the believer to understand that purity does not come from outer observance. Most of his conflicts with the Pharisees were about this point. But in this Beatitude, it appears that he is speaking precisely about ritual purity. He literally says, "Lucky the cleansed". This is, of course, exactly what his listening audience would have expected.

For hundreds of years before Yeshua arrived on earth, religious purification rituals dominated the Jewish religion. The distinction between "clean" and "unclean" was so important that it was inseparable from belief in God. Unless a Jew was clean in the ritual sense, he could have no part in the ceremony of worship. The idea of religious cleanliness permeated life, affecting birth, food, sacrifice, sex, disease and death. Old Testament instructions in Leviticus were central to the practice of the Jewish faith. Although these purification rituals were intended as a guide for living, they gradually became a nearly impossible burden as they were expanded and elaborated. The term "Pharisee" meant "separated one". The Pharisees separated themselves from ordinary people for the purpose of consecration to the ritual observance. Some Pharisees believed that obedience to every one of these laws was essential in order to be accepted by God. This was the quintessential "checklist" religion. Do everything right and God is obligated to give you spiritual credit.[25]

## Ritually Right

Let's take a journey back to that day and listen to the comments.

---

[25] Paul's letter to the Galatians is an argument about why these rituals do *not* affect God's acceptance of a person and are *not* required in order to experience God's grace, but that is *not* the same as saying that these rituals and the other instructions in Torah have no place in the Kingdom.

Malachi was standing at the side of the crowd now. After hearing those opening announcements, he and his friends were about ready to leave. Imagine the utter audacity of this so-called prophet! All of those "common" people being told they were lucky. What nonsense! Just thinking about them gave him a chill. They were all so defiled. It was hard to even be here. There were so many of them who might touch him.

Then he heard Yeshua continue. But this time his ears perked up.

"Lucky the cleansed".

"Finally", thought Malachi. "At least he's getting something right. No more of this stupidity about those beggars and worthless scum. It's about time he made clear who is really accepted.

But, what? Wait a minute. What did he say? Cleansed in the heart? No, impossible. No one can do that! It's just too much to ask! Everybody has some secret. Every one knows their own hidden failures. How can he possibly mean ritually pure in heart? Ritually cleansed on the outside, yes, I can manage that, but on the inside? Who can make that happen?"

Yeshua must have aroused the interest of the religious practitioners with this Beatitude. He started out saying exactly what they wanted to hear. It's all about being "clean". The word is deliberate. Everyone in that audience knew exactly what he was saying when that word came from his mouth. Follow the rules – all of them – meticulously, stringently, continually.  But suddenly the context changed. "Clean in the heart".  What rules were there for being clean in the heart?  Suddenly it didn't matter how many times you washed your hands, how many wordy invocations you recited or how many sacrifices you brought to the altar.

Even more incredible was the fact that Yeshua wasn't saying those rituals were going to be replaced by another set of rules.  He was saying something far more unbelievable.  He was saying that none of the rituals were good enough if they did not produce a clean heart.  But they **couldn't** make a heart clean. Nothing on earth could!  It was the book of Job all over again:  "Can a man be more pure than his Maker?"[26]

The concept was not new.  David told us who would stand in the holy place.  Only the man "who has clean hands and a pure heart" has any hope of standing before God (Psalm 24:3-4).  The Hebrew words are *naqiy* and *bar*.  "Clean hands" means "free of guilt" and "pure heart" means "exonerated of blame".  Who could ever make such a claim?  Even the mighty prophet Isaiah was struck with fear in the presence of the holy God as he said, "Woe is me for I am a man of *unclean* lips".  The verdict is in.  Every Jew knew the decision before the bailiff read it.  The prophets only confirmed (Jeremiah 17:9) what had been true since Noah. Every man's heart was evil (Genesis 6:5). No one could stand before the Almighty and claim to have a clean heart.

As if that weren't bad enough, Yeshua went on to say that the ones who had no guilt and were free of blame in their hearts would *see* God.  That must have put incredible *fear* in his audience.  Even Moses

---

[26] Job 4:17

nearly made a fatal mistake when he asked to see God. Seeing God was the recipe for annihilation. No one could see God and live. Two impossibilities in the same announcement. This man had to be crazy!

## Clean Today

Is it any different today? I really don't think so. I was at a business gathering yesterday. A group of men began to talk about religion. One lawyer said to me, "I used to feel uncomfortable about all that miracle stuff about Yeshua. But we had a speaker who is an expert on the history. It's really just fables. Now I know that religion is just about how to live right. All I have to do is be a good person. I can do that. I feel a lot better." It's so much easier to have clean hands than a clean heart.

My wife grew up in the Catholic Church. I went to an Anglican school. We were surrounded by ritual. Count so many of these. Walk like this. Say these words. Make these motions. *Visible* purity. Could I do everything just right? It only took lots of practice. It is so much easier to have a checklist rather than a moral inventory.

What would happen if Yeshua visited our Sunday church service? Would he follow the "rules" of worship? Would he bow at the right times, raise his hands, lower his head, pass the offering plate, listen to the sermon about giving more money to the building fund? Or would he search for the pregnant teenager or the junior-high kid on drugs? Maybe he would mention the resentment in my soul, or the lie that you told your spouse? Would he ask for another chorus to give us time to respond to the same altar call we heard last week with the same "I see that hand" salesmanship while the deacon deletes the porno website on his computer and his wife gossips about the new neighbor. We are comfortable with a religion of rules because it is so "obvious" – another way of saying that it is under our control. We want to be seen as we wish to be, not as we are. The matter of the heart is so difficult to reveal. If I ever even think about telling you my secret sins, I quickly force the feeling into the closet and slam the door shut. Fear. That's what a "clean heart" really means. Fear of being exposed. Say another "Hail Mary" and hope it goes away.

Not only does this Beatitude bring fear in its opening statement, it brings fear in its conclusion. I fear being cleansed of heart because I know just how much of a hypocrite I am. And I fear seeing God because I know that my unholiness will scorch me to death.

During our studies of the first five Beatitudes, we saw that Yeshua proclaimed "Lucky" those whom the world would consider the least likely candidates. Instead of the religiously respectful, Yeshua said the spiritually destitute were fortunate. Instead of the jubilant, Yeshua announced happiness to those who grieved. Instead of victors, Yeshua said the oppressed should jump for joy. Instead of the prosperous, Yeshua announced the luck of the chronically needy. Instead of the rightful winners, Yeshua tells us happiness belongs to those who give up their rights. Now Yeshua says something even more amazing. Now he says that the lucky people are those with clean hearts. And we already know that **not one single person in the world** can make such a claim. Each Beatitude applies joy to a small group of the vast majority. This one delineates a group of *zero*!

The First Century audience was shell shocked, I'm sure. As Yeshua spoke, some of the listeners may have been thinking that his pronouncements were for them. Some were undoubtedly destitute in spirit – hoping beyond hope for God's intervention. Some were certainly hungry for righteousness, some feeling under God's thumb, some willfully setting aside their rights. But no one could have expected this. It is the equivalent of "let him who is without sin cast the first stone". All have come short of the glory of God. Nevertheless, Yeshua stood and proclaimed the luck of the clean in heart in a world where every person is dirty.

The Pharisees must have been the first to shudder. They certainly knew that outward rule-keeping wasn't nearly enough. Yeshua sliced through their pretensions with God's razor. Unless your heart was cleansed, you were in the category of the miserable. Outward ritual observance was nothing but whitewash on gravestones. Inside the casket, the body was still rotting. Yeshua conveyed the same thought when he said, "Unless your righteousness *exceeds* the righteousness of the Pharisees". Who could ever manage that? Pharisees spent their entire lives trying to keep all the rules.

This Beatitude, however, was no relief to the rest of the audience either. Even if they were not caught up in the ritual behavior of checklist religion, it took only a moment's reflection to know that they were not clean. They might eat the right foods, go to the right assembly, say the right prayers, but nothing they did was going to produce a heart clean enough to see God. This time Yeshua's announcement put the fear of judgment in everyone.

Modern religion is no different. Have we changed our moral bankruptcy by converting "sin" into the need for psychological counseling? Aren't "guilt" and "blame" simply politically incorrect terms for the "religiously challenged"? Apparently Yeshua did not think so. Our sin is serious business. In fact, it is the most serious business in the world. It is so serious that it affects everyone on the planet. It looks like no one is jumping for joy about this announcement.

## Dirty Luck

So, who are the lucky ones in this Beatitude? There can be only one answer – Lucky those who have experienced the creation of a **new, clean** heart. They will see God because God saw them first. You bet they are lucky. They are ecstatic! Nothing on earth can match what only God could do for them. MasterCard can pay the rent for the sanctuary, the cost of the hymnals and the price of the communion. But a clean heart is priceless!

Remember that a Beatitude is not a bestowal of favor. It is not a "blessing" that implies one party grants a gift to another party. A Beatitude is really a macarism – an announcement of an existing state – the description of the bliss of being lucky. Yeshua is not saying, "You are blessed *because* you have a clean heart and that gives you a ticket to see God". He is saying, "You lucky people who have clean hearts". In other words, it is the clean heart that demonstrates luck. And, by the way, says Yeshua, this kind of luck also means you are going to see God.

## Seeing God

Let's look at that phrase "you shall see God". The verb is *opthanomai*. Here it is future tense, middle voice. The middle voice in Greek tells us that this is an activity that has particular importance to the subject. It is not "you will see" but rather "you will see for yourself". We have already noted that "seeing God" was considered a fearful thing. Since everyone is unworthy, standing face-to-face before absolute holiness meant certain destruction. In light of this fact, what could Yeshua possibly mean?

Most commentators regard this phrase as eschatological. They interpret it as an announcement about the *eventual* encounter with God in heaven. Purity of heart qualifies a person to be in God's presence, a fact that will not be fully realized until we leave this world. This interpretation easily moves us out of the realm of ritual purity and into the realm of moral purity. But, of course, Yeshua isn't addressing *moral* purity. He is talking about *ritual purity of the heart.* He is talking about a heart that comes into the presence of God without spot of blemish *now!* How does that happen?

There is another theme that flows from this metaphor. Yeshua repeats it over and over in his ministry. It is this: only the man whose life has been made righteous by God (pure in heart) has the eyes to see God's hand in the world today. This is the same idea that is captured in the often-repeated proclamation, "He who has ears, let him hear". In order to perceive the presence of God, one must be cleansed. If this is what Yeshua has in mind, simply stating it was evidence that the external ritual purity of the culture was inadequate. External purity could never prepare a man to stand before God nor would it allow men to observe the presence of God in their midst. After all, Yeshua was standing right in front of them and they did not see him for who he was.

*Opthanomai* helps us to understand this subtlety. It does not mean simply to observe – to visually record what passes before the eyes. It implies that what is visually recorded is *actually understood.* This is the difference between *opthanomai* and *blepo* (the Greek verb that means simply having the faculty of sight). Yeshua is saying that the pure in heart rejoice because they truly see. The character of their inner spiritual eyes has been changed so that their perception discovers God in what they observe. They see *and understand*. In this sense, seeing itself is paradoxical. It is entirely possible to "see" and not "see" at all. Only those who look with invisible eyes actually see – and what they see is the invisible God.

## The Paradox of Sight

*Paradoxa* – the Greek word behind paradox – means "one opinion beside the other". Here we see two sets of "one beside the other" thoughts. The first is the paradox that luck is the blissful condition of those with clean hearts. Clean enough to stand before the Lord of hosts. And not one single person in the world has a pure heart like that. So, if we are to experience this kind of bliss, we will have to be changed into something we are not – clean. The second paradox depends on the first. We can only see *after* we are changed because in order to see God, we must have the eyes of a clean heart. Look all you want with the eyes of outward religiosity and you will never see what is right in front of you. But become pure in heart and the whole world will suddenly become a visual panorama of God in the midst.

The impossibility of being clean is no more impossible than seeing God. Neither can be accomplished by human effort. Both occur in the moment of God's choosing. Both are a matter of *luck*! *Makarioi*, my friends. *Makarioi.*

Yeshua stood before that audience and told the entire human race that we are lucky; that we are in a state of bliss about something we have never had – because God was going to give it to us. The number of people who shared this happiness because of their own cleansing was *none* at all. But the number who could share this happiness because of the Savior was everyone.  All the dirty laundry would be white as snow.  That happiness was the state of seeing God. Now and in the future.  Darkly, then face to face.

Lucky those with cleansed hearts.  Their eyes see God.

**Do You See?**

1.  Is your heart clean or are you just being religious?

2.  Do you see God?

3.  Does He see you – and do you let Him?

4.  How lucky are you to be dirty before Him?

# $\mathcal{D}$angerous

**"Blessed are the peacemakers: for they shall be
called the children of God"
Matthew 5:9**

Who doesn't want to have peace in life? Just a little
time off from the daily grind. No more arguments
with the kids or the spouse. Just getting along with
the boss or the employees. Wouldn't it be nice?
Peace and tranquility. Life as a vacation.

But it isn't usually like that, is it? Life seems to
bounce us from one crisis to the next. Just when you
think you've got the finances figured out, someone
near to you has a terrible health issue. Maybe your
health is great, but you can't seem to get the bills
under control. You work all your life to get ahead,
and when you arrive, she says that she doesn't feel
appreciated any more and wants a divorce. You get a
promotion, but the market takes a bath. The family is
great but the neighbor starts a rumor that destroys
your reputation at church.

Peace, peace, just give me some peace. We all want it.
But it seems so hard to get. The Beatles knew how
we all feel when they said, "Give you everything I've
got for a little peace of mind".

Unfortunately, Yeshua is not going to make things
easier with this Beatitude. This macarism is not for
those who want peace but for those who *make* peace.
And you can't make peace unless you are in conflict
and ready to put yourself at risk. If you're going to be
a peace*maker*, someone is going to shoot at you.

"Peacemakers" is a term constructed from more than one Greek word – *eirene* (peace) and *poeio* (to make or do). For the first time, we have a Beatitude that incorporates a necessary positive action by the subject. In the other Beatitudes, Yeshua pronounces luck on people whose defining characteristic is their present passive condition or negative relinquishing action. They appear to be destitute, grief-stricken, afflicted, painfully deficient, unclean and losers. But now Yeshua says that something positive must be done in order to belong to this group. The one who is "blessed" here must *make* peace.

A great deal of material has been written about the peace-making activity of the Christian. Rick Warren devotes an entire chapter to the idea that restoring relationships is an essential part of God's purpose for the believer.

> If you want God's blessing on your life and you want to be known as a child of God, you must learn to be a peacemaker. Yeshua said, "God blesses those who work for peace, for they will be called the children of God."[27]

Nicoll echoes the thought of most commentaries when he says that this word does not mean merely those who are peaceable or peace loving, but rather those who are "the active heroic promoters of peace in a world full of alienation".[28]

Finally, Foerster says that this word:

---

[27] Rick Warren, *The Purpose Driven Life*, (Zondervan, 2002), p. 153.
[28] W. Robertson Nicoll, The Expositor's Greek Testament, (Eerdmans, 1990), Vol. 1 p.100.

denotes the establishment of peace and concord between men. The reference is to those who disinterestedly come between contending parties and try to make peace. These God calls his sons because they are like Him.[29]

It seems that this Beatitude fails to comply with the pattern of a macarism. On the surface, there is no *sacred paradox* in this statement. If you go about trying to make peace between men, God recognizes your efforts. It's a bit more than commonsense because God's blessing is usually not part of our commonsense language. But it looks like a far cry from the upside-down backwards thinking of the previous announcements of Yeshua. Is this really all that Yeshua is saying?

Let's return to the First Century audience. How would they have understood Yeshua's words?

First Century Israel was a melting pot of major cultural influences. The Greek influence arrived as the backbone of intellectual society, the foundation of Roman law and the cultural heritage of the common trading language of the entire Mediterranean world. The Roman influence made its presence felt in the politics of oppression and the power of military occupation. And, of course, the Jewish population held on to its own roots through its religion and customs, dating back through the ages to Father Abraham. All three of these powerful forces were at work in the lives of the people of Yeshua's time. All three of them affect the concept of peace.

For the Greeks, the idea of peace is not about harmony between men. Peace is not about relationships at all. It is rather a description of an

---

[29] Foerster, TDNT, Vol. II, p. 419.

*abnormal state of affairs* lasting for a designated time. The Greeks believed that strife and conflict were essential elements of life. This can be seen in their fables, games, gods and history. Peace was a negative concept. It was simply the *lack* or *absence* of war, whether external or internal. Peace was the intermission between the acts of real life.

This negative non-relational understanding is completely reversed in the Hebrew concept of peace. The Greek word *eirene* was used to translate the Hebrew word *shalom*. But *shalom* is first and foremost a concept about relationships between men. In fact, its fabric is so entrenched in human relations that it is used as a common greeting like "How are you today?" Jews greeting each other passed mutual blessings with the word "Peace" (*shalom*). They still do this today. In this capacity, it carries the meaning of a wish of well-being, especially material prosperity. It signifies bodily health and stability in life's affairs. But it is always couched within the framework of Almighty God. Peace is ultimately a gift of God. David expresses the connection between material blessings, national security and spiritual salvation in Psalm 85 – all a result of the outflow of God's lovingkindness (the Hebrew word is *hesed* – a critical word in the understanding of the covenant relationship between God and His people). In thirteen verses, David shows that God is the responsible agent of favor, liberty, forgiveness, mercy, revival, salvation, truth and prosperity – a summary of the relational concept of peace. David says, "righteousness and peace have kissed each other". This can only be true if *God* provides peace since righteousness is ultimately the sole work of God.

There are three categories of meaning to the Hebrew word *shalom*: well-being between men with an emphasis on material and bodily prosperity, peace between peoples and nations and finally, salvation accomplished by God. In the Old Testament, this last sense, salvation, looks toward the future. The prophet Isaiah demonstrates the connection between salvation and peace in that famous verse:

> For a child will be born to us, a son will be given to us; And the government will rest on His shoulders;
> And His name will be called Wonderful Counselor, Mighty God, Eternal Father, Prince of Peace (Isaiah 9:6)

When the Hebrew Old Testament was translated into Greek so that it could be read by converts throughout the Roman Empire, the word *eirene* was used to translate *shalom*. But we have already seen the *eirene* had nothing to do with relationships between men while *shalom* had everything to do with relationships between men and God. This means that the Greek word *eirene* in the New Testament is *not* used in the way it is used in classical Greek. It must be understood in the way it is used in the LXX, the Greek of the Old Testament. "Peace" came to mean a state of well-being that described the entire condition of men. This peace was internal and permanent protection and salvation because it was given by God. Even death could not disturb it.

Another influence made its way into the meaning of the word "peace". First Century Jews revered the teachings of the rabbis. These commentaries on Old Testament literature added the idea that "peace" was more than a gift of God to men – it was actually a description of the state of affairs between men and God. According to rabbinical teaching, God was in conflict with all ways of the flesh. Peace and strife were polar opposites describing the condition of men before God. Men play an essential role in the balance of peace and strife. If they obey Torah, they set aside strife with God and enjoy God's peace. If they disobey Torah, only strife and punishment can result. Peace becomes a word that directly describes the relationship between men and God.

The last idea of peace for the first Century Jew was the Roman influence. This was not a linguistic influence. It was the ever-present, visible influence of brutal occupation. Rome stood against everything that the Jews believed, from culture to religion. Rome ruled with an iron fist, an in-your-face power that reminded every Jew of the lack of peace in life. The Jewish population longed for that sweet taste of freedom and the refreshing breeze of peace.

When Yeshua opened his mouth and said, "Lucky those making peace" many senses of the word would have come to mind. While the previous Beatitude (pure in heart) seemed to exclude everyone, this Beatitude seems to include everyone. The Greek word is so broad in meaning that every segment of those listeners could nod approval. But as soon as we understand how each group may have responded, we see a contradiction emerge.

The common people of his audience would have immediately thought of their own well-being and prosperity. Peace for them meant good fortune, good heath and good times. But it was beyond their grasp. They were the *am ha-aritz*, the people of the land, the masses of poor. They might greet each other with *shalom*, but they had never experienced the blessing of *shalom*. There was no peace for them in their world.

The political activists would have thought of the bliss for those who were not in conflict and war. And, of course, Israel was an occupied and oppressed country. Making peace by removing the brutal suppression of Rome would have been bliss indeed! But there was no end in sight for the tortures and brutality of Roman rule. Every uprising had been squelched. The roads were lined with crucifixions. The inhumanity of man toward man was the order of the day. Peace was only a dream, available when sleep overcame the nightmare of being awake.

Still another interpretation could have sprung to mind. The rabbis in the crowd would certainly have thought of peace with God. They preached ritual purity and practice in an effort to turn away the wrath of God and find peace with Yahweh. But even here peace could not be found. Because some rabbis believed that God judged man on the basis of fulfillment of the Torah, no man could claim personal peace in front of a holy God. Under the weight of the Law, it was always possible to unintentionally overlook some action that should have been performed (a sin of omission) or, in the final moments of life, discover some sin that had not been cleansed. These rabbis lived in constant fear that God would find some fault they had overlooked. They could never be certain of final salvation. Peace was just a wish that mocked the reality of moment-by-moment fear of failure in obedience.

Finally, no Jew could have missed the allusion to the prophecy of the coming Messiah. It had been instilled in them for hundreds of years – waiting for the Messiah who would usher in the golden age of peace. Isaiah, Jeremiah, David and Daniel all foretold a coming age of God's peace through the reign of the Messiah. Hope against hope, yet to be realized. Hundreds of years of waiting, waiting, waiting. And still God was silent. Could the Messiah finally be coming on the stage? Even though this must have been in their minds, nothing about Yeshua would have given them reason to believe that he was the one. He shunned military involvement. He opposed the religious rulers. He remained isolated from the mainstream. About Yeshua only one thing was certain – confusion.

None of the meanings of peace seem to have applied to the crowd who listened that day. Is this the sacred paradox of Yeshua's macarism? I don't believe so. Even though in each case the meaning of peace seems to be just beyond the reach of the audience, there is no paradox here. Peace was no more available in the First Century than it is today, and surprisingly, for many of the same reasons. This is not paradoxical. It is just disheartening.

To see the paradox here, we need to look at the use of this Greek word in the rest of the New Testament. What we find is this: *eirene* is almost always used in the deeper sense of salvation, but rarely used to describe the relationship between God and man. It is salvation in the rabbinic sense – the end of strife with God. It is almost always a present condition, not a future hope. The New Testament understands peace as the cessation of hostility with God through salvation provided by the Christ. Peace describes the state of the believer, assured of God's grace, content with God's authority. Peace is directly connected with righteousness, safety, love, grace and glory.

> God's peace is independent of outside conditions and is the fruit of an objective, real salvation with God.[30]

---

[30] Spiros Zodhiates, *The Complete Word Study Dictionary: New Testament* (AMG, 1992), p. 520.

Peace in the New Testament is the **normal** state of affairs. War with God is not the intention of this world. Paul contrasts peace with confusion. Peace is normal; confusion abnormal. Peace is the result of God's salvation provided to men. God guarantees the security of citizens of His Kingdom. It is the opposite of affliction. Peace is the normal condition of life. In the New Testament, peace and life are opposed to strife and death. Peace, then, is a word that summarizes the life of those who are citizens of the Kingdom of Heaven. At last, they have clarity, security and contentment as God intended, under God's protection and guarantee.

Probably no one in the crowd on that hill experienced this reality of peace. Nevertheless, the paradox is not that they wished for peace but didn't experience peace. The paradox is connected to the combination of "peace" with "maker". The paradox is that only those who are presently giving up this hoped-for reality reflect God's character and God's peace.

Let's say that again. Everyone wants peace. That is to say, everyone wants to experience life where they themselves enjoy peace. *But not the peacemaker.* The peacemaker is one who actually gives up personal harmony and tranquility in order to put himself at risk for the sake of peace. He stands in harm's way because he attempts to bring someone else's conflict to an end. You can't be a peacemaker without stepping into a war. You can't be a peace-maker if you watch from the sidelines, waiting for well-being to come to you, waiting for political freedom to be given to you, waiting for God's wrath to be turned from you, waiting for the Messiah to make things better for you. Peacemakers are active. They engage in battle – not to fight but to diffuse, not to aggravate but to appease, not to control but to counsel. But peacemakers are in and of themselves a

108

paradox. The very thing they long for is exactly what they relinquish. In order to bring peace, they must become part of the strife. They must step into the fire.

Yeshua says, "Lucky those who give up their peace for the sake of someone else's peace". This is a paradox, all right. What we learn from the four meanings of peace is that giving it up seems to be the last thing anyone would want to do. It certainly seems contradictory to say that luck falls on those who deliberately step out of tranquility into conflict. Should this verse really be translated as the New Living Translation suggests?

God blesses those who work for peace

Does this mean that God blesses anyone who puts himself in harm's way for the sake of peace? Does it mean that God therefore, automatically, blesses Jimmy Carter, the Peace Corp., Colin Powell, General Tommy Franks, the NYPD and dozens of other "peace-makers"? Yeshua never suggested such a broad application with any other Beatitude. On closer examination, every other Beatitude had a much more restricted audience than first appeared to be the case. Why would that change now?

I believe that the only way to really see the paradox of this macarism is to read it backwards. To understand this macarism, we must start with the phrase "called sons of God". Two concepts are important. "Sons of God" means those who are designated God's children. They are children in the sense that they exhibit a family resemblance. They are adopted into God's family. The term "sons" here emphasizes the parental care toward those who *yield* their lives to the formation of God's character in

109

them. They are like God in His benevolence, self-sacrifice and mediation.

The "sons of God" are those who are being conformed to the image of the Son of God. The action of stepping into conflict in order to bring peace is exactly what God does. By being peacemakers, these people relinquish their own tranquility and harmony as a reflection of God's self-sacrifice for them. They work toward reconciliation. They follow the same pathway trod by the Son who left the tranquility and harmony of divinity (the peace of heaven) to become a slave, be tormented and abused and finally executed as the One who stood between those in strife.

This is another example of mirror image behavior. John tells us that we love because He first loved us. We mirror His action. We reconcile because He first reconciled us. Mirror action. The hidden reality is that the one who spoke these words to the world was the ultimate example of self-sacrificing on behalf of peace. The one who told us about the bliss of the peacemaker *is* the peacemaker, the one we executed.

As the crowd heard this Beatitude, they felt the longing for peace – a God-given desire for what God intended to be normal. Some may even have understood that real peace comes only when someone gives up tranquility and engages in reconciliation. But those who jumped for joy knew that they were face-to-face with the One who exemplified ultimate peacemaking. They jumped for joy because they were no longer at war, and they couldn't wait to help others end the conflict as well.

The second word is *klethesontai*. It is from the root *kaleo*, which means "to call". Here it is passive. So, we should translate it as "are regarded or accounted as". The designation is not something they earned .

It is a description of their character by someone else. When they act as mirror images of God's self-sacrifice, they are viewed as though they have God's nature. Yeshua made it all very clear when he said if you do this to the least of these, you do it as though you were doing it to me. In other words, peacemakers step into God's shoes. That's why they are described as God's children. They act the way their Father does. They do not earn the title "sons of God" because they act as peacemakers. They act as peacemakers because they reflect what it means to live as God's sons.

Now we can answer the question: "Does God bless anyone who steps into harm's way for the sake of peace?" The answer is YES but also NO. It's YES because many human actions reflect God's values but do so without acknowledging the divine-human mirror. When we love unselfishly, we reflect God's love even if we don't know it. When we show mercy, we reflect God's mercy. When we comfort, we demonstrate God's care. God's image, however tarnished, is reflected in being human. Even if we do not worship our Creator, the innate character of His values resides in us because we are made in His image.

But the answer is also NO. God does not bless anyone who steps in harm's way. God's idea of peacemaking is not the same as Man's. It is for this reason that the New Testament tells us "not by might or by power, but by my Spirit". Peacemaking is ultimately from God, but only those who act *on God's behalf and in God's stead with God's method* really know the joy of self-sacrifice for another. The dim reflection of the divine image is there in every peacemaking act. But the "jump for joy" *makarios* excitement can only belong to the one who knows his own peace is but a prelude to God's peace for all – in every sense of the term:

Well-being
End of hostilities
Salvation
The reign of the Messiah
All at once. All together.

The peacemaker knows his own peace is built on self-sacrificial relinquishing of peace. He is just reflecting what was given to him. The peacemaker who is called a son of God enters the conflict without any of Man's weapons. He is not from the United Nations security force. He is not with the Marines. He does not wear a badge. He is armed with only the assurance of God's love for the end of conflict. And for him, that is more than enough to defeat any army.

The sacred paradox is this: the peacemaker joyfully relinquishes his own peace for the sake of ending strife between men for no other reason than reflecting the character of his Father. The peacemaker knows God's peace is found in standing in conflict. The peacemaker knows that he can bring peace only by letting go of peace. And God recognizes that this decision is just what He does.

Incredibly lucky those deliberately stepping into their Father's shoes in efforts to bring peace between men. God considers them symbols of His family image.

**Are You Making Peace?**

1. Where are you stepping into the battle to bring about peace for others?

2.  What wounds have you received on God's behalf?

3.  Are you looking for peace or are you providing peace?

4.  Do you realize that God trusts you to deliver peace wherever you are?

# $\mathcal{D}$riven

**"Blessed are those who have been persecuted for the sake of righteousness, for theirs is the kingdom of heaven." Matthew 5:10**

Our contemporary view of persecution is often associated with Christians in other countries who are tortured for their faith. We recall the terrible persecutions of the Romans, the demonically driven rage of Islam in the 7th Century and, of course, the Inquisition – the church persecuting its own. But these images create a problem. Yeshua spoke to a first century crowd of peasants and poor, beggars and believers, religious and rejected. Where are the tortured in that crowd? There was no one in chains, on the rack, staked to the ground or being stoned. If Yeshua meant to speak about those who would be tortured by lions and sword, they certainly were not present that day.

This indication of something amiss in our interpretation gets a bit larger when we realize that this last Beatitude shares one significant element with the first Beatitude. It is the only other Beatitude in the *present* tense. In fact, it contains exactly the same concluding phrase as the first Beatitude ("theirs is the Kingdom of Heaven"). This is not a mistake. Yeshua clearly intended to apply this teaching to that audience on that day, not to some future group of believers. The fact that his statements become timeless insights into the inner workings of God's world does not entitle us to ignore what he must have intended his original audience to understand.

So, if it is fairly certain that no one present on that day was in the process of being tortured, what group did Yeshua have in mind? Answering this question reveals the incredible depth of this Beatitude, a depth that transforms it from a statement of religious zeal into a declaration of God's grace.

A state of bliss describes those who are connected to the Greek verb *dioko*. Of course, we won't understand what makes this a sacred paradox until we know the meaning of this verb. There are two uses of *dioko*. The non-religious use means, "to set in motion" or "to impel". It is a short step from that idea of the second use, "to persecute". In the New Testament, the second meaning predominates.

Unfortunately, we will need to do a bit of grammatical digging before the treasure in this word is revealed. In Yeshua's statement, the verb is a perfect passive participle. The grammatical construction is important. First, it is in the perfect tense. The perfect tense in Greek expresses an action that has been completed in the past but has continuing consequences into the present. This allows us to see the first characteristic of these lucky people. Apparently, they have been persecuted for a long time, and the effects of that persecution have not stopped.

Secondly, the verb is passive. The active voice implies that the subject of the sentence is the one acting. But the passive voice implies that something is done to the subject. Persecution has been put upon these people. They did not go looking for it. They did not encourage it. Others inflicted it upon them.

Finally, the verb is a participle. A participle is a verb that acts like an adjective. Adjectives modify nouns. That means participles describe additional characteristics of nouns. Here is a participle, but where is the noun? We have to add it to make sense of the Greek words. The Greek text literally reads, "Lucky the being persecuted". So we add "those" or "the ones". The action itself makes them the subject of Yeshua's statement.

Can you see the importance of this distinction? We often feel as though we deserve divine rewards because we have endured some insult or injury at the hands of unbelievers. We look at this Beatitude and decide that God owes us blessings for our trials. But if our "persecutions" are finished, we are not the ones Yeshua is addressing. Yeshua is talking to those whose lives are at this very moment characterized by oppression and persecution. There is an older classical sense of this word that comes into play. It is "to accuse". Yeshua is speaking to those who are presently suffering under accusation, who are at this moment being driven out, who are oppressed by unjust punishment. The results of this persecution have not ended. Their lives are under the thumb of those who judge them.

Yeshua did not teach in Greek. He taught in Hebrew. Matthew and Luke translated his Hebrew words into Greek when they wrote their respective gospels. Matthew wrote to a Jewish audience. His translators were incredibly careful to pick Greek words that would reflect the original Hebrew sense of Yeshua's statements for a Hebrew audience. Today, we must decipher what word Yeshua most likely used by a process of linguistic dissection. The LXX becomes an indispensable aid in this effort because it shows us which Hebrew word or words were translated with the Greek word *dioko*.

What we discover is that the Greek concept is tied to the Hebrew word *radaph*. This word is unique to

Biblical material. It almost always carries the meaning of pursuit with the intention of revenge or harm. This is a description that carries two interrelated motions. One group flees while another chases. Persecution is about one party attempting to free itself from harm while another party tries to inflict harm.

Yeshua qualifies this chase with an important addition: "For the sake of righteousness". We have encountered this concept in the fourth Beatitude. The concept of righteousness is closely linked to the Hebrew Torah. From the ten commandants to the instructions given in Deuteronomy and Leviticus, God's rule governed all aspects of life. The Old Testament consistently affirms that God's rule is the proper order for all life. God Himself is the embodiment of righteousness. The Torah is simply an expression of His character as the Holy God. God is *The* Ruler Who establishes the Law based on what He knows to be true because it is the expression of His very Being.

Some of the rabbinical clergy believed that right standing in front of God (righteousness) was based on outward pious behavior. In other words, they thought that if they kept all the rules, their human efforts would result in a balance in their favor and God would reward them. For this reason, these scribes and Pharisees were meticulous about rule keeping. This was incredibly serious business. Their lives hung in the balance, both in this world and the next. These religious leaders laid the impossible burden of legal perfection on their followers. In fact, they considered the common people beneath God's grace because these ordinary human beings were incapable of maintaining the exactitude of the religious law.

This culture of religious piety drove grace away from those who needed it most. Yeshua attacked this belief and practice as nothing more than self-righteousness. In concert with most of the Jewish sages, Yeshua claimed that no man could possibly *earn* favor with God. Righteousness was a gift, not a reward.

Let's consider the statement in this Beatitude from this perspective. The crowds who heard Yeshua on that day knew full well the meaning of being driven away from God by a group who pursued them. Sometimes the clergy were the persecutors. They took every opportunity to inflict great religious burdens on God's children. They demanded perfect compliance to the religious system of traditions and interpretations. They reconstructed righteousness as a measure of achievement. In the process, they inflicted harm upon God's message of grace. Their insistence on the practice of human self-worth literally made war with God. And those who did not conform to their demands were driven away with proclamations of religious revenge. The very people whose desperate cry precipitated the response of God were being driven away from God's free gift of right-standing by the religiously correct.

There is another facet to the use of *dioko* that cannot be overlooked. When it occurs in this second religious sense, it always implies the guilt of the oppressor. This nuance suggests that the action is not justified persecution. This is not proper punishment for unholy acts. It is quite the opposite.

We look back across the centuries and, with perfect hindsight, see that this process was opposed to God's plan of faith. We fault the legalistic Pharisees just as Yeshua did. But our hindsight is of no value whatsoever if it does not open our eyes to the present reality of legalism. Yeshua is speaking not only about torture and suffering. He is speaking about a culture that places religious behavior ahead of grace.

*Dioko* always implies that the persecutors are guilty. They are guilty of distorting the righteousness of God. They are guilty because they have altered God's holy character and sovereign exercise by filtering it through human requirements. This is just as true for religious rules as it is for physical torture. Paul reiterated this essential teaching of the gospel when he said that the believer has been put to death to *all* legalism (cf. Romans 7:4). There are *no* human rules that stand between Man and God.

This should give us great concern. Consider your own religious environment. It might be helpful to take paper and pen and write down all of the expectations, rules and regulations that govern your relationship with God. Is your worship governed by an expected structure? Is your giving constrained by the stewardship committee or the offering envelopes (or your own debate about ownership)? Are your social behaviors driven by the need for "religious approval?" Who determines your style of prayer or your hymns of praise? Or the clothes you wear or the cut of your hair? Unfortunately, it's not just the religious application that persecutes.

*"And they tie up **heavy loads**, and lay them on men's shoulders, but they themselves are unwilling to move them with so much as a finger." Matthew 23:4*

The Greek combination *phortia barea* paints a very clear picture. Shipping freight. Take a trip to the docks. Watch those gigantic cranes lifting massive cargo. Now imagine it all on your back. It's a weight none of us can bear.

Yeshua is talking about the weight of religious and cultural expectations. We could just as easily add the weight of all the obligations put on our own lives. Yeshua observed that those who were preoccupied with rules and rituals were most often the ones who gladly shifted burdens onto others but who routinely avoided taking any responsibility on themselves. How many of us have gone through that experience? Seeing the boss becomes a dreaded experience because it means that the workload just got bigger. What a difference it would make if the boss came to us and said, "How can I help lift the load you are carrying today?"

We all have the option of being a taskmaster or a servant. It really doesn't matter if you are at home, school or work. You can always dump another burden on someone if you wish. Or you can take another approach. You can get into the business of lifting burdens. You can become part of the relief mechanism instead of the oppressing machinery.

Yeshua led by lifting. He made lifting a principle of living in order to take the burden from our shoulders. Being a servant means carrying the freight for someone else. In this Beatitude, Yeshua makes it clear that the persecuted are not only those who are beaten and tortured for their proclamation, "Yeshua is Lord." The persecuted are those who have been denied access to God's grace because of religious legalism. The persecuted are those who have been driven out of God's house because they didn't dress right or because they didn't say the right things or because their lifestyle didn't fit. The persecuted are those who have been excluded from fellowship with God because they didn't say the right prayers or take the right posture, because they didn't give enough or didn't look the part. Wherever men have erected barriers between God and His children, Yeshua applies this Beatitude.

Of course, this does not mean that anything goes once we experience God's acceptance. Paul makes it very clear that we are not to engage in sinful behavior just so God can apply more grace. That isn't the point of this Beatitude. God does have a code of conduct. It has been articulated in Torah. As Moses says, "This is not too difficult for you." We can keep to God's path and He expects us to do so. But keeping to the path is not about *earning salvation.* It is about making myself as available as possible so that God might use me for His purposes in any way He chooses – and ultimately it is about living differently so that my demonstration of His instructions becomes an attraction to others.

Now we can see why the last Beatitude models the first. The last Beatitude completes a circle. We began by noticing that the first Beatitude is built around a *present tense* sense of desperation. All of the remaining Beatitudes are focused on the *future* resolution of God's actions. But when we reach the last of these sacred paradoxes, we return to the present tense again. It is a *present tense* Beatitude because the acts of persecution that Yeshua has in mind are acts that drive away God's response to desperation. We do not have to wait for political change to be persecuted for the sake of righteousness. All we have to do is raise a question about the requirements of church practices or beliefs to see the witch hunt begin. Yeshua came to proclaim God's unmerited favor. Wherever men insert *any requirement* between desperation and grace, persecution occurs. And the persecutor is *always guilty.*

If we recall the radical discovery that the kingdom of heaven is not a reward but rather an answer, we will see why Yeshua returns to this identical concluding thought. Yeshua is God's answer to our cry for grace. Anyone who finds grace in spite of the interference of persecutors can only experience one emotion – sheer happiness! Just like the other Beatitudes, this is not a conditional statement of merited reward. I do not earn my place in God's kingdom by enduring persecution. It is not about effort at all! It is about discovery! It is discovering that God's righteousness is for me in spite of the religious legalism that attempts to circumvent that discovery. It is about the happiness I find when I realize that God has answered. No human burden, no religious demand can remove that joy from me once I have tasted its sweet refreshment. I will no longer be under the yoke of the oppressor, even if that oppressor wears a cleric's robe. Desperation and persecution are in the same family. If I am desperate for God, many men will attempt to drive me away from Him. But God answers. Oh, happy day! How lucky can a man be?

Yeshua proclaimed that God's grace was an unconditional invitation to everyone. If we add anything to this invitation, we harm God's message. Yeshua taught that God draws all who respond to this invitation. If we qualify the ones He draws, we harm God's message. Yeshua announced that the only condition of salvation was repentance. If we add burdens to this process, we harm God's message. And finally, Yeshua commanded that the only measure of a follower was submission to Him. Wherever men demand anything more or tolerate anything less, they step outside God's righteousness.

This is perhaps the most sobering of all the Beatitudes. When we realize that it is not about torture chambers and cattle prods, when we see that it is about obscuring the simple clarity of grace, we should shudder under its judgment. As we discovered in the first Beatitude, God's kingdom arrives precisely because He hears and answers the cries of His desperate children. If we interfere with that process, we are the persecutors.

How often have we let our religious comfort zones dictate the announcement of God's desire to demonstrate grace? Do we do good to our enemies? Do we go the extra mile? Do we turn the other cheek? Do we treat *all* of our assets as loans from God? Have we sacrificed our own agendas on the altar in order that we might live only according to His ways?

Perhaps we are on the other side of the persecution coin. How many times have we lessened the demand of Lordship in order to gain membership? How often have we overlooked the smallest sin in order to gain personal advantage? Are white lies acceptable to us? Is contempt? Is arrogance? Every time we stand between God and His grace for someone else, we are the persecutors.

**How are you being driven?**

1. What drives you? Make a list.

2. Do any of these drivers separate you or others from the experience of God's grace?

3. Are any of your drivers out of alignment with God's instructions?

4. Are you ready to put your agendas on the altar so that others can find the Lord of life?

# The Final Paradox

In this study we have discovered that each of the Beatitudes presents us with a sacred paradox.

We found that the destitute in spirit are the reason God's kingdom has arrived.

We found that those who grieve are the open doors for God's comfort to the world.

We found that those afflicted under God's sovereignty discover God's promised allotment.

We found that those who are chronically deficient in righteousness are given the righteousness they lack.

We found that those who give up justice discover the basis of their own pardon.

We found that those who have received a clean heart have eyes able to see God.

We found that those who relinquish peace discover they reflect God's character.

We found that those who stand for grace no matter what call for the Kingdom's arrival.

Each of these points to God's bedrock values. They are nothing like the values we prize in this world. In God's world, the things that matter most are:

Desperateness
Brokenness
Affliction
Emptiness

Losing
Insufficiency
Sacrifice
Perseverance

These are the values of the new Kingdom. These are the ways that God conducts His affairs with men. Insofar as we avoid these values, we turn our backs on God's ethics.

But there is one more paradox. It is found in the entire collage of adjectives about these "lucky ones". Let's look once again at the results of *makarios*.

God's kingdom arrives
God's comfort reaches us
God's order prevails
God's righteousness is provided
God's pardon is given
God's hand is seen
God's peace reigns
God's instructions are followed

The final paradox is that the man delivering these sacred paradoxes is himself the fulfillment of each of the stages of *makarios*. He is the living sacred paradox. He is the arrival of the Kingdom, the one who comforts, the fulfillment of God's order, the reason from righteousness, the pardon completed, the visible God and the end of our strife. Yeshua is *makarios*.

Yeshua announced a new world – the world of upside-down, backwards thinking. But it is only upside-down and backwards from our perspective. In God's view, the conditions of the "rejoicing ones" are perfectly normal.

Desperate before God
Mourning life's brokenness
Trusting in God's sovereign control
Accepting the gift of righteousness
Rejoicing in God's pardon
Looking for God's handiwork
Making peace on God's behalf
Standing for His grace

And Yeshua is the conduit of every one of these heavenly values.

Lucky are the desperate for God; Yeshua brings the kingdom of heaven. His arrival is the answer to the pleadings of the destitute for God. He is the essence of the kingdom – God's reign on earth and in heaven. "I have come that they may have life".

Lucky are those in mourning; Yeshua is the resurrection and the life. "If any man die in me, yet he shall live". His death ends the power of death. He brings what the grieving need – the assurance of life.

Lucky are those afflicted under God's grace; Yeshua has come to "release the captives". The fellowship of suffering with Yeshua is the weight of glory, the joy of the Lord's communion. His body is broken for you. His blood is spilled for you. He was oppressed and afflicted, a man of sorrows for you. "My burden is light".

Lucky are those who are chronically deficient before God; Yeshua brings right-standing. Righteousness is satisfied. Hunger for God is fulfilled. Yeshua is our bread of life.

Lucky are those who don't get what they deserve; Yeshua provides what justice would have demanded and insures our pardon. "If the Son shall set you free, you shall be free indeed".

Lucky are the cleansed; Yeshua is the one who does the cleansing. "I am the way, the truth and the life." "Your sins are forgiven".

Lucky are those who give up their peace for the sake of others; they are following their Master. "A new commandment I give to you, that you love one another as I have loved you."

Lucky are those who are driven to grace no matter what stands in their way. Yeshua has heard them. "For this I came into the world."

Yeshua.

He showed us what it means to live completely for God.

He wept over the world's brokenness and separation.

He gave his life on the basis of "thy will be done".

He was the means of our righteousness.

He removed the penalty we deserved to grant us pardon.

He made us see God in our fallen world.

He ended our war with the Father.

He delivered the message of grace.

Yeshua is the paradox of all paradoxes. He is the man in the middle, the man of another world living in the midst of our groaning creation, the author and

127

finisher of our faith.  What he announced was God's strategy of redemption, in proclamations of rejoicing. God hears our cry and sends His Son.  God sees our grief and His Son brings comfort.  God announces His control and His Son confirms it.  God designates us righteous by His Son's obedience.  God pardons us because His Son takes the blame.  God shows us His love through the life of His Son.  God announces peace with the sacrifice of His Son.  God responds to our pursuit of Him by letting His Son be driven out for us.

Rejoice, jump for joy, you incredibly lucky one.

***Makarios*** **all you who acknowledge life as paradox.  You are welcome in God's world.**

# APPENDIX 1

## The Beatitudes in Luke

Luke 6:20-23 contains the only other recording of the Beatitudes. However, the content differs from the statements in Matthew in two important ways: first, only four of the eight Beatitudes in Matthew are found in Luke, and secondly, those that are found in the passage in Luke are altered.

We could consider this variation nothing more than the difference between an eye witness (Matthew) and an interviewer of those who were there (Luke). From a purely historical perspective, this explanation is entirely probable and reasonable. However, the explanation is *theologically* difficult, especially for one who holds a high view of inspiration.

Let's look carefully at the differences and see if we can resolve them.

### The introduction in Luke and Matthew

Luke's statements are in the second person while Matthew's are in the third person. There is no essential difference in meaning associated with this change. The second person plural may carry a more intimate tone since the passage in Luke suggests that Yeshua is addressing his disciples rather than a wider audience. It is worth noting that the audience of disciples certainly included considerably more than the twelve. The Greek word *mathetes* generally means "pupil or learner" but in the New Testament it carries the idea of a follower of Christ (or of John the Baptist). There were many people who were followers of Yeshua. As followers of a rabbi, they adopted his teachings and made him the guide for their conduct. These are the people he addresses in the Sermon on the Mount. The statements of the Beatitudes are for them, although it is quite likely that there were many others in the audience who were not his disciples. The Sermon on the Mount occurred early in the ministry when large crowds followed Yeshua. It was only after the unsuccessful attempt to push Yeshua into the role of an earthly conqueror that the crowds disappeared. Luke's perspective seems to be an address to a tighter circle. But this is to be expected. Luke was not an eye witness to the event and his information had to be gathered from interviews of those who were present. If he interviewed one or more of the apostles, he would have naturally gained the same perspective they had.

We should notice, however, that Matthew's account makes the same distinction. Matthew 5:1 says that Yeshua, seeing the crowds, moved to a spot on the hillside. His disciples (followers) came to him. Even though Luke recounts the choosing of the twelve just before the teaching on the hillside, Luke agrees with Matthew that a great crowd surrounded Yeshua (verse 19) and sought him out. What Yeshua said to his followers, whether they are designated as the twelve or the larger group, was certainly overheard by this crowd. More importantly, the impact of Yeshua's statements was meant for all who had ears to hear even if the immediate audience was much smaller. Luke's use of the second person plural may be nothing more than a result of his sources. There is nothing here that is incompatible with Matthew.

Now let's look at the details of the text.

Luke 6:20 and Matthew 5:3

**"in spirit"**

The first of Luke's Beatitudes seems to present a problem. Matthew has *"Makarioi* (lucky) the poor in spirit" while Luke has only *"Makarioi* the poor".

Notice that both accounts choose the same word for "poor" – *ptochoi*. Certainly this choice is dictated by the deeper meaning of *ptochoi* and the distinction between *ptochoi* and *penes*. The real question is why does Luke omit "in spirit". Perhaps the answer can be found in the usual association of the word *ptochoi* with religious assumptions.

Norval Geldenhuys suggests that because Yeshua addressed only his followers, he was already addressing those who "do not seek their wealth and life in earthly things, but acknowledge their own poverty and come to Him to seek real life".[31] Geldenhuys asserts that the ""poor" of this type *are* already members of His kingdom".[32] In other words, Geldenhuys suggests that the concept behind Matthew's distinction "in spirit" is already contained in the usage of *ptochoi* when it is specifically addressed to Yeshua's followers. There was no need to specify "in spirit" because this added distinction was already present in the religious use of *ptochoi*.

Geldenhuys is not thoroughly convincing. He must assume that those who heard Yeshua say, *"Makarioi ptochoi"* has already adopted the perspective of abject destitution in their spiritual condition and therefore needed no further qualification. But this assumption seems entirely out of character with the behavior of the disciples. They continue to debate

---

[31] Geldenhuys, Norval, *Commentary on the Gospel of Luke* in *The New International Commentary on the New Testament* (Wm. B. Eerdmans, Grand Rapids), 1951, p. 210.
[32] *Ibid.*

concerns about power, status and influence and the gospels all portray these men as confused and spiritually unenlightened until after the resurrection. It seems presumptuous to claim that Luke's term indicates followers who already had deep spiritual commitment.

Nevertheless, Geldenhuys points us in the right direction. Luke interviewed his sources long after the awareness of Yeshua's true meanings had become evident. By the time Luke wrote, there was little doubt about what Yeshua had in mind because all of the apostles now had the distinct advantage of hindsight. They could legitimately include the spiritual connotations of *ptochoi* when discussing the event with Luke because they were now aware of those implications. And if they communicated this idea requiring Luke to find an appropriate Greek word, they may have connected the spiritual attitude of desperation for God as part of the concept of *ptochoi*.

This argument might relieve the tension for the passage in Luke, but it then begs the question, "Why did Matthew feel compelled to introduce the distinction "in spirit" in his report?" The question is intensified by the following consideration: If Yeshua said, "*Makarioi* the poor in spirit", is it reasonable that Luke's source would *leave out* this distinction? And if Yeshua said only "*Makarioi* the poor", why would Matthew deliberately *add* this distinction?

I believe that the answer is found in the ethnic background of the two authors. In spite of the fact that both gospels are transmitted to us in Greek, Yeshua did not speak Greek. Yeshua spoke Hebrew. So the actual word he used was not *ptochoi* but a Hebrew word that has been translated as *ptochoi*.

This presents a significant linguistic problem because, except for a very few words and phrases, all of the New Testament is written in Greek. Therefore, we have no direct way to determine what Hebrew word Yeshua used. Nevertheless, the preponderance of evidence suggests that Hebrew was his native tongue so we must at least construct plausible linguistic associations between *ptochoi* and Hebrew equivalents.[33]

We can begin with an explanation of the passage in Luke. Newman and Stine point out that *ptochoi* "is used in the Septuagint to translate Hebrew words that mean not only "poor" and "needy" but also "broken in spirit" and "humble."[34] Examination of the LXX shows that *ptochoi* is used to translate the Hebrew *'ebyon* (needy) in 1 Sam. 2:8 and *ani* (afflicted, humbled) in 2 Sam 22:28, the cry of the poor (in parallel with the cry of the afflicted using both *'ebyon* and *ani*) in Job 34:28 and *ani* in Job 36:6. *Ptochoi* is *'ebyon* (needy) in Ps. 11:6 in the LXX (12:5 in the English translation), *ani* (poor) in Ps. 68:30 LXX (69:29 English), *'ebyon* (needy) in Ps 71:12 LXX (72:12 English).

There is an important link between *ptochoi* and *penes* in many Psalms where the Hebrew linked words are *ani* and *'ebyon* (as in Ps. 85:1 LXX, 86:1 English). The combination of *ani* and *'ebyon* is linked to "brokenhearted" in 109:16 English (108:16 LXX).

---

[33] While it has been *de rigueur* to claim that Yeshua spoke Aramaic, this long-held view is crumbling under the weight of archeological and linguistic evidence. See in particular Biven and Blizzard, *Understanding the Difficult Words of Jesus*, 2nd edition.

[34] Newman, Barclay M. and Stine, Philip C, *A Handbook on The Gospel of Matthew* (United Bible Societies, New York), 1988, p. 108.

The Hebrew word *dal* is connected in the combination of *dal* and *'ebyon* in Isaiah 14:30.

Of special note is the translation of Isaiah 61:1:

> The Spirit of the Lord is upon me to bring good news to the afflicted.

Yeshua quotes this passage at the opening proclamation of his ministry. In this verse, the Hebrew word *anaw* (in the same word group as *ani*) is translated by *ptochoi*.

These passages give us ample evidence that the LXX usage of *ptochoi* contained within it the concepts of *'ebyon* and *ani* (*anaw*), with clear parallel connections to *dal*. Since Luke was Greek and was writing to a Greek speaking audience, in all probability he relied on the LXX as his reference for Hebrew concepts. Therefore, he would have naturally felt that *ptochoi* incorporated the necessary emphasis on spiritual orientation capturing the nuance that Yeshua had in mind. Any reference to *'ebyon*, *ani*, *anaw* or *dal* in Hebrew would have led Luke to *ptochoi* as the proper Greek translation. We can conclude that the Greek word *ptochoi* is an umbrella concept when compared to the Hebrew language. All three Hebrew words, *ani*, *'ebyon* and *dal* are translated or linked to this single Greek word. By using *ptochoi*, Luke captured all of the nuances found in the Hebrew. It was therefore unnecessary to further delineate for his Greek audience the extension "in sprit". The thought was already there.

Now that we have answered the question, "Why did Luke use only the word *ptochoi* rather than *ptochoi* in spirit?", we must address the other side of the coin – "Why did Matthew *include* the clarification "in spirit"?" The answer is found in the fact that *ptochoi* is a larger umbrella word that any of the several possible Hebrew words it could translate.

Hebrew gives us several possible choices for the thought behind the Greek word *ptochoi*. These are: *anaw, dal, rash* and *'ebyon*. Each of these words carries the sense of "poor" but there are distinctions between them that help us determine which one is more likely to have been used by Yeshua.

*Anaw* is primarily associated with the idea of affliction through oppression. The verbal form (*ana*) is used more than two hundred times. It describes the actions of an enemy, pain inflicted by bondage, suffering through war and the distress of slavery. Theologically, the word is used to describe pain and suffering as the vehicle that leads to repentance. As an adjective, *anaw* "stresses the moral and spiritual condition of the godly as the goal of affliction implying that this state is joined with a suffering life rather than with one of worldly happiness and abundance."[35] *Anaw* is intended to produce humility.

*Dal* is an adjective that means poor or weak. However, it is often used as a noun. This word emphasizes the lack of material worth. It is used to describe those who are socially weak and materially deprived. God protects these people and promises them justice. Nevertheless, *dal* is rarely used to describe spiritual poverty. Coppes provides the following distinctions: "Unlike *ani*, *dal* does not emphasize pain or oppression; unlike *'ebyon*, it does not primarily emphasize need and unlike *rash*, it

---

[35] Coppes, Leonard J., *Theological Wordbook of the Old Testament*, (The Moody Bible Institute of Chicago, Chicago), 1980, p. 682.

represents those who lack rather than the destitute."[36]

*Rash* is used only thirty-two times in Scripture. It describes the common plight of the lower classes – to be without resources or social standing. It is used metaphorically to describe unworthiness. Psalm 82:3 tells us that God will answer the needs of this group and provide them with justice.

Finally, *'ebyon* places significance on need as opposed to affliction or weakness. While there may be a wide variety of reasons for the poverty of these people, their social status is always a concern with God. The Mosaic code protected these people. They are even called God's favored ones (Isaiah 25:4). The majority of the occurrences of this word are in the Psalms where the word expresses the sense of those whose only remaining help must come from God. Psalm 72:4 tells us that those who are needy in this way are God's true spiritual people. Their cry is the basis of God's action (Psalm 12:5 and 70:5).

It is speculation, of course, but I believe that this last word, *'ebyon*, is the Hebrew concept that lies behind the Greek translation *ptochoi*. I dismiss *anaw* because *anaw* is undoubtedly the Hebrew thought behind the Beatitude, "*Makarioi* the meek." *Anaw* is about forced affliction with the intention of producing humility. Yeshua directs our attention to this connection in his statement about the happiness of those who are oppressed (meek = Greek *praüs*). The fact that the Beatitude about the meek is a quotation from Psalm 37:11 leaves little doubt concerning the Hebrew background.

---

[36] *Ibid*, p. 190.

136

*Dal* focuses attention on weakness and lack, not on destitution. I find that *dal* is much closer to the concept behind the Beatitude, "*Makarioi* the ones hungry and thirsty". The emphasis of that Beatitude is on chronic need and continued insufficiency, not on total destitution.

Likewise, *rash* is found in the context of weakness, unworthiness and lack of resources. For the same reasons that *dal* is rejected, I do not find *rash* a probable candidate.

This leaves *'ebyon*. But there is more in favor of this concept than simply process of elimination. *'ebyon* is primarily about physical destitution and spiritual bankruptcy. Those who are *'ebyon* can ultimately find relief only in the action of God. They are His special protected ones and it is that awareness that enlightens them to see His handiwork. *'ebyon* are the *ptochoi* in spirit. They are precisely the ones who are crying out for the kingdom because they have no other avenue for justice. Furthermore, *'ebyon* is a consistent theme of the Psalms, a source that we know undergirds several Beatitudes.

Let us suppose that this is the concept Yeshua has in mind when he spoke the Hebrew phrase that became translated as "*Makarioi* the *ptochoi*." We can imagine a reasonable explanation for the use of this word in Luke. Luke was not at the event. He had to gather his information by interviewing. If the person or persons that Luke interviewed conveyed the Hebrew expression to Luke as a Greek word, they could easily have used *ptochoi* as the only necessary Greek equivalent because they understood the religious connections between *ptochoi* and *'ebyon*. They would have had years to think about the real meaning of Yeshua's statements. When they wanted to convey this Hebrew concept to a Greek-speaking writer, they made the distinction between *ptochoi* and *penes* but found it unnecessary to make any further delineation. Luke's intended audience would associate *ptochoi* with those who were desperate physically *and* spiritually.

But what about Matthew?

The puzzle about Matthew is also answered by paying attention to the intended audience. Matthew writes to a Jewish audience. If the readers of Matthew's gospel where primarily Jews, then translating Matthew's Hebrew into Greek would need to distinguish precisely which Hebrew concept was implied by the broader Greek word *ptochoi*. In order for Matthew's account to tell his readers that Yeshua had *'ebyon* in mind, the translator needed to add "in spirit" as a way of more precisely defining the broader Greek term *ptochoi*. This addition delineated more accurately what Yeshua said when Yeshua used the Hebrew expression already distinguished from *anaw*, *dal* and *rash*. Matthew's account was required to expand the Greek concept in order to capture the precise Hebrew idea of *'ebyon* without leaving open the possibilities that Yeshua may have had one of the other Hebrew words in mind. This was critical to an audience familiar with the four Hebrew words. Matthew's Greek would have been inadequate in capturing the precise meaning had it not specified the spiritual connection to *'ebyon* by adding "in spirit". This delineation was not important to Luke because Luke's readers already associated *ptochoi* with the idea of spiritual destitution.

Does this mean that Matthew and Luke disagree? Of course not. Each account is translating an original Hebrew concept for a different reader. Does this mean that there are errors in one or the other gospel? Again, no. What we see is the attempt by two different writers to capture a statement uttered in another language. We should expect to have variations in the translation if the writers do not share the same linguistic heritage or target audience.

### "of heaven"

We are not out of the woods yet. Matthew reports that Yeshua said, "theirs is the kingdom of heaven" while Luke reports "yours is the kingdom of God". The change from third person to second person has been discussed. But what do we do with "heaven" and "God"? While there is no difference in meaning, Yeshua obviously did not say *both* things. Either Yeshua said "kingdom of heaven" or he said "kingdom of God". And this could imply that one or the other writers reported it incorrectly.

To resolve some of this problem, we need to return to Hebrew. Yeshua may have used the word *shamayim* (Hebrew "heaven"). But there are reasons why he probably did not use the word *Yahweh*. If Yeshua used this name, he would probably have been accused of blasphemy. The accusation would have been based on the ritual avoidance of any mention of God's name for fear of violating the second commandment. In fact, this prohibition was so strong that Jews routinely substituted the word *adonai* (Lord) whenever they encountered either of the other words, even in the reading of Scripture. It seems particularly unlikely that he would have violated the protocol at the opening of a great teaching message on the ethics of God's rule.

There is another factor to consider. Matthew writes to Jews. Matthew's purpose is to show Jews who are not yet believers that Yeshua is the Messiah, the anointed one. It is Matthew's account that reports the inoffensive expression "of heaven" rather than

139

the potentially offensive "of God". If Matthew wanted to convey the radical nature of Yeshua's claims about happiness within God's rule, he would have no reason to introduce a divisive issue concerning the use of God's name. Matthew focuses on the point of the *makarios* – the kingdom has arrived. For Matthew, "of heaven" is merely an evasive synonym, clearly understood by his audience.

Luke, on the other hand, writes to Gentiles who have no religious prohibition against using the word *theou* (God). In fact, Luke has every reason to convey the meaning that this is not some "other worldly" kingdom of the heavens. It is quite specifically God's kingdom.

Since the essential meaning of the terms "kingdom of heaven" and "kingdom of God" are identical, the reason that Yeshua's statement is reported differently must be explained by pointing to the entirely different audiences of each writer.

This argument does not finally resolve the problem. It cannot be *finally* resolved because we will never know what word Yeshua really used. But we do know that the concept he expressed is captured in both of these Greek phrases. And we see that it makes sense that the authors tailored their translations to fit the audiences they had in mind.

### Luke 6:21 and Matthew 5:6

Matthew's fourth and second Beatitudes are found in Luke 6:21. Here we have problems with the order, the exclusion of Matthew's third Beatitude and finally, with the text itself.

It seems reasonable to suggest that the cardinal order in Luke is different simply because of the author's construction and preference. Whether the order should be Matthew's or Luke's has little bearing on any question of historicity. Both authors simply assume that Yeshua spoke these words. Neither one makes any point about the order in which they were spoken except for Matthew's Hebraic *inclusio*, the repetition of the present tense and the same conclusion in the first and last Beatitude.

A more difficult issue is Luke's exclusion of "*Makarioi the praeis* (meek)", the third Beatitude in Matthew. As we noted in discussion of that Beatitude, some modern translations consider Matthew's third Beatitude an addition made by a later scribe, principally on the basis that it is not found in Luke and the fact that it seems to be an extension of the thought in the first Beatitude. I have shown that Matthew's third Beatitude is not an extension of the first and therefore, is not to be viewed as a scribal extension. But that still leaves the question of exclusion in Luke.

The exclusion issue is really not as significant as we might think. Luke does not claim to report *all* that Yeshua said. He simply claims that what he does report is what Yeshua said. There is no reason to believe that exclusion presents a difficulty. Even Matthew's account does not claim to be exhaustive.

The real issue is once again the alteration in the actual wording. Luke's version is "*Makarioi hoi peinontes nun* (happy you hungering **now**)" rather than Matthew's "*Makarioi hoi peinontes kai dipsontes ten dikaiosunen* (happy you hungering **and thirsting for righteousness**)". We see two issues. First, Luke adds "now" and, secondly, Luke omits "and thirsting for righteousness".

The omission is less problematic than the addition. As we have already argued, Luke does not claim to report *all* that Yeshua said. And since Matthew and Luke agree exactly on the opening thought of this Beatitude, we have confidence that Yeshua did say (in Hebrew) the thoughts contained in that Greek phrase. If we recall the deeper meaning of Matthew's fourth Beatitude, we know that the concepts of hunger and thirst carried significant religious implications for the Jewish audience. Matthew's inclusion of this material fits his literary purpose. He wants his Jewish readers to grasp the full impact of Yeshua's deliberate references to their own Scriptural history. Luke simply does not focus on this element because the religious history of the Jews was not as significant to his mostly Gentile audience. The same argument used to suggest resolution to the variation in wording of the first Beatitude applies here. The differences can be accounted for by considering the purpose and the audience.

But the addition of *nun* (now) presents a slightly different problem. To this point we have shown that Luke's *omissions* of material found in Matthew makes sense because of the differences in gathering the information (eyewitness vs. interview), audience (Jew vs. Gentile) and purpose (Yeshua is the Messiah vs. Yeshua is the Son of God). But now we face the problem in reverse.

Matthew records his version as an eyewitness. It is much more reasonable to assume that he records the fuller version because he does not have to rely on other people to gather his material. Luke's sources may have easily left something out, as we have suggested in prior discussion. But here we have a situation where it appears as if the eyewitness account *omits* a crucial idea. We must either supply a reasonable explanation why an eyewitness would omit this thought, or we must show why Luke would deliberately *add* something to the text.

Is it more reasonable to focus on Matthew's omission or on Luke's addition? Once again, we must attempt to read back through the translation to the word Yeshua used. The Hebrew word *ra'ab* is a noun that refers to acute hunger. This word is found in the Old Testament context of punishment and discipline brought about by God's providential removal of food (Jeremiah 32:24, Isaiah 5:3 and Amos 8:11). The verb form (*ra'eb*) describes a person with a chronic condition of the lack of life's necessities. As we mentioned in the examination of the Matthew text, every Jew knew that God was the source of life's food and that God could withdraw that essential as a means of punishment or discipline. The context of the word *ra'eb* included the *present reality* of being famished. Any Jew who understood *praüs* within the context of Old Testament religious history would instantly know that this condition was not a hypothetical suggestion or a past experience. *Ra'eb* was *now*!

Reiling and Swellengrebel[37] suggest that Luke uses *nun* to place emphasis on the contrast between present hunger and future satisfaction ("you will be satisfied"). If this is so, we should notice the same emphatic contrast is contained in Matthew's translation, only in Matthew's case, *ra'eb* is already emphatically present tense.

Luke's readers did not share the same religious linguistic heritage. While Matthew could safely assume his audience understood the sense of

---

[37] Reiling, J. and Swellengrebel, J. L., *A Handbook on The Gospel of Luke* (United Bible Societies, New York), 1971, p. 269.

immediacy in this translation, Luke added the Greek adverb *nun* in order to insure that his readers understood the same immediacy.

Once again we see that a reasonable explanation for this variation can be found in the translation from Yeshua's Hebraic statements to the written Greek found in Matthew and Luke. All that is required here is a *reasonable* explanation, not an exhaustive proof. It is worth noting that the text of the remainder of this Beatitude in both Matthew and Luke is identical (with the exception of the change in person).

**"weep now"**

Finally we come to the Beatitude "*Makarioi* those mourning", found in Luke as "*Makarioi* you that weep now." Our resolution of the addition of *nun* (now) by Luke in the previous Beatitude applies here as well. Matthew's translation of Yeshua's thought clearly places the activity in the present tense. Yeshua is addressing those who at this moment are experiencing mourning. Matthew's Greek gospel chooses the verb *pentheo* to express this thought. Luke uses the Greek verb *klaio*. These words are synonyms. Both verbs express the emotional and spiritual actions of grief. Both words are found in both writers with no essential difference in meaning. Luke's added *nun* once again emphasizes the contrast with the remainder of the Beatitude. Matthew employs the same contrast in his choice of *pentheo* in the participle form – present tense active and immediate.

**"you shall laugh"**

The end of this Beatitude in Luke presents the last puzzle. Luke uses the Greek verb *gelao* (to laugh or be merry) while Matthew uses *parakaleo* (to call to one's aid, to comfort and encourage). There is some connection between the two activities. Those who experience comfort and encouragement after grief may perhaps laugh as an expression of new joy. But the connection does not seem obvious and the two words carry us in different directions.

If we attempt to reconstruct the expression that Yeshua used, we have two possibilities based on these Greek words. They are *naham* (to comfort) and *sahaq* (to laugh or rejoice).

If Yeshua used the Hebrew expression *naham*, he would have recalled a rich heritage. Comfort is often associated with death. Psalm 23:4 tells us that God's presence comforts us and removes the fear of death. Psalm 69:20 uses the word in a prophetic allusion to the crucifixion. Psalm 71:21 ties *naham* to the idea of resurrection. God is the true source of comfort (Ps. 86:17, 90:13, 106:45). God's law is a present comfort (Ps. 119:52). Compassion and comfort go hand-in-hand (Ps. 135:14). In the passive verb form, *naham* takes on the same meaning that Matthew supplies with the Greek word *paraklethesontai* (they shall be comforted). This is a consolation brought by someone else to those in grief.

Luke's version uses the Greek *gelao*, a word that would normally translate *sahaq*. The combination of "weep" and "laugh" in Luke seems to be a deliberate referral to Ecclesiastes 3:4.

> A time to weep and a time to laugh
> A time to mourn and a time to dance

If Luke used the LXX as his reference to Hebrew, he would have seen *sahaq* translated as *gelao* in this verse. And if Yeshua were deliberately referring to the comment of the Teacher in Ecclesiastes, the

145

combination of weep and laugh would have emerged. This connection is also supported by Luke's report in 6:25 when Yeshua says:

> Woe to you who laugh now, for you shall mourn and weep.

If we look at the other uses of *sahaq*, we find an important variation in the translation in Job 19:7 and Jeremiah 20:8. Job 19:7 translates *sahaq* with the Greek verb *krazo* (cry out). Jeremiah 20:8 translates *sahaq* with the Greek *gelao* but the sense is certainly not laughter but anguish. Both uses point to *sahaq* as a cry of intense suffering, not laughter. It is possible that *gelao* as a translation of *sahaq* contains a shadow of a connection to comfort for mourning, not peals of laughter. We should understand the word as a description of mood and emotion, not necessarily a description of vocal rejoicing. In this regard *gelao* shares a nuance with *paraklethesontai*.

Nevertheless, I am not able to fully resolve this difference in the same manner as the treatment of the other variations between Luke and Matthew. I see tangents where the two linguistic concepts share nuances, but I do not find the overlapping linguistic evidence that we discovered in the other phrases. Perhaps it is only a matter of writer's preference. Perhaps there is a conceptual commonality that we no longer understand. That Yeshua uttered the statement translated by both of these men is beyond doubt. Exactly what he said in Hebrew that resulted in the choice of *gelao* and *paraklethesontai* may never be known. I only hope that this contribution has helped.

# APPENDIX 2

## *Makarios* in the LXX and the New Testament

### Genesis

30:13  Then Leah said, "Happy am I! For women will call me happy." So she named him Asher.

### Deuteronomy

33:29  "Blessed are you, O Israel! Who is like you, a people saved by the LORD,  Who is the shield of your help, and the sword of your majesty!  So your enemies will cringe before you, and you shall tread upon their high places."

### 1 Kings

10:8 "How blessed are your men, how blessed are these your servants who stand before you continually *and* hear your wisdom.

10:9 Blessed be the LORD your God, who has delighted in you and set you on the throne of Israel; because the LORD loved Israel forever, therefore He has made you king, to do justice and righteousness."

### 2 Chronicles

9:7 "How blessed are your men, how blessed are these your servants who stand before you continually and hear your wisdom."

9:8 Blessed be the LORD your God, who has delighted in you, setting you on his throne as king for the LORD your God; because your God loved Israel establishing them forever, therefore, He has made you king over them, to do justice and righteousness."

**Job**

5:17 "Behold, happy is the man whom God reproves, so do not despise the discipline of the Almighty."

**Psalms**

1:1  How blessed is the man who does not walk in the counsel of the wicked, nor stand in the way of sinners, nor sit in the seat of scoffers!

2:12  Do homage to the Son, that He not become angry, and you perish *in* the way, For His wrath may soon be kindled. How blessed are all who take refuge in Him!

32:1  *A Psalm* of David. A Maskil. How blessed is he whose transgression is forgiven, Whose sin is covered!

32:2  How blessed is the man to whom the LORD does not impute iniquity, And in whose spirit there is no deceit!

33:12  Blessed is the nation whose God is the LORD, The people whom He has chosen for His own inheritance.

34:8  O taste and see that the LORD is good; How blessed is the man who takes refuge in Him!

41:1  For the choir director. A Psalm of David. How blessed is he who considers the helpless; The LORD will deliver him in a day of trouble.

65:4  How blessed is the one whom You choose and bring near *to You* To dwell in Your courts. We will be satisfied with the goodness of Your house, Your holy temple.

84:4   How blessed are those who dwell in Your house! They are ever praising You. Selah.

84:5   How blessed is the man whose strength is in You, In whose heart are the highways *to Zion!*

84:12   O LORD of hosts, How blessed is the man who trusts in You!

89:15   How blessed are the people who know the joyful sound! O LORD, they walk in the light of Your countenance.

94:12   Blessed is the man whom You chasten, O LORD, And whom You teach out of Your law;

106:3   How blessed are those who keep justice, Who practice righteousness at all times!

112:1   Praise the LORD! How blessed is the man who fears the LORD, Who greatly delights in His commandments.

119:1   Aleph. How blessed are those whose way is blameless, Who walk in the law of the LORD.

119:2   How blessed are those who observe His testimonies, Who seek Him with all *their* heart.

127:5   How blessed is the man whose quiver is full of them; They will not be ashamed When they speak with their enemies in the gate.

128:1   A Song of Ascents. How blessed is everyone who fears the LORD, Who walks in His ways.

128:2  When you shall eat of the fruit of your hands, You will be happy and it will be well with you.

137:8  O daughter of Babylon, you devastated one, How blessed will be the one who repays you With the recompense with which you have repaid us.

137:9  How blessed will be the one who seizes and dashes your little ones Against the rock.

144:15  How blessed are the people who are so situated; How blessed are the people whose God is the LORD!

146:5  How blessed is he whose help is the God of Jacob, Whose hope is in the LORD his God,

## Proverbs

3:13  How blessed is the man who finds wisdom And the man who gains understanding.

8:34  "Blessed is the man who listens to me, Watching daily at my gates, Waiting at my doorposts."

20:7  A righteous man who walks in his integrity— How blessed are his sons after him.

28:14  How blessed is the man who fears always, But he who hardens his heart will fall into calamity.

## Isaiah

30:18  Therefore the LORD longs to be gracious to you, And therefore He waits on high to have compassion on you. For the LORD is a God of justice; How blessed are all those who long for Him.

32:20 How blessed will you be, you who sow beside all waters, Who let out freely the ox and the donkey.

56:2 "How blessed is the man who does this, And the son of man who takes hold of it; Who keeps from profaning the sabbath, And keeps his hand from doing any evil."

## NEW TESTAMENT

### Matthew (other than the *Makarioi* in Matthew 5)

11:6 "And blessed is he who does not take offense at Me."

13:16 "But blessed are your eyes, because they see; and your ears, because they hear."

16:17 And Jesus said to him, "Blessed are you, Simon Barjona, because flesh and blood did not reveal *this* to you, but My Father who is in heaven."

24:46 "Blessed is that slave whom his master finds so doing when he comes."

### Luke

1:45 "And blessed *is* she who believed that there would be a fulfillment of what had been spoken to her by the Lord."

6:21 "Blessed *are* you who hunger now, for you shall be satisfied. Blessed *are* you who weep now, for you shall laugh."

6:22 "Blessed are you when men hate you, and ostracize you, and insult you, and scorn your name as evil, for the sake of the Son of Man."

7:23 "Blessed is he who does not take offense at Me."

10:23 Turning to the disciples, He said privately, "Blessed *are* the eyes which see the things you see,"

11:27 While Jesus was saying these things, one of the women in the crowd raised her voice and said to Him, "Blessed is the womb that bore You and the breasts at which You nursed."

11:28 But He said, "On the contrary, blessed are those who hear the word of God and observe it."

12:37 "Blessed are those slaves whom the master will find on the alert when he comes; truly I say to you, that he will gird himself *to serve,* and have them recline *at the table,* and will come up and wait on them."

12:38 "Whether he comes in the second watch, or even in the third, and finds *them* so, blessed are those *slaves.*

12:43 "Blessed is that slave whom his master finds so doing when he comes."

14:14 "and you will be blessed, since they do not have *the means* to repay you; for you will be repaid at the resurrection of the righteous."

14:15 When one of those who were reclining *at the table* with Him heard this, he said to Him, "Blessed is everyone who will eat bread in the kingdom of God!"

23:29 "For behold, the days are coming when they will say, 'Blessed are the barren, and the wombs that never bore, and the breasts that never nursed."

## John

13:17 "If you know these things, you are blessed if you do them."

20:29 Jesus said to him, "Because you have seen Me, have you believed? Blessed *are* they who did not see, and *yet* believed."

## Acts

20:35 "In everything I showed you that by working hard in this manner you must help the weak and remember the words of the Lord Jesus, that He Himself said, 'It is more blessed to give than to receive.'"

## Romans

4:7 "BLESSED ARE THOSE WHOSE LAWLESS DEEDS HAVE BEEN FORGIVEN, AND WHOSE SINS HAVE BEEN COVERED.

4:8 "BLESSED IS THE MAN WHOSE SIN THE LORD WILL NOT TAKE INTO ACCOUNT."

14:22 The faith which you have, have as your own conviction before God. Happy is he who does not condemn himself in what he approves.

## 1 Corinthians

7:40 But in my opinion she is happier if she remains as she is; and I think that I also have the Spirit of God.

## 1 Timothy

1:11 according to the glorious gospel of the blessed God, with which I have been entrusted.

6:15  which He will bring about at the proper time—
He who is the blessed and only Sovereign, the King of
kings and Lord of lords,

## Titus

2:13  looking for the blessed hope and the appearing
of the glory of our great God and Savior, Christ Jesus,

## James

1:12  Blessed is a man who perseveres under trial; for
once he has been approved, he will receive the crown
of life which *the Lord* has promised to those who love
Him.

1:25 But one who looks intently at the perfect law,
the *law* of liberty, and abides by it, not having become
a forgetful hearer but an effectual doer, this man will
be blessed in what he does.

## 1 Peter

3:14 But even if you should suffer for the sake of
righteousness, you are blessed. AND DO NOT FEAR
THEIR INTIMIDATION, AND DO NOT BE TROUBLED,

4:14 If you are reviled for the name of Christ, you are
blessed, because the Spirit of glory and of God rests
on you.

## Revelation

1:3 Blessed is he who reads and those who hear the
words of the prophecy, and heed the things which are
written in it; for the time is near.

14:13   And I heard a voice from heaven, saying, "Write, 'Blessed are the dead who die in the Lord from now on!'" "Yes," says the Spirit, "so that they may rest from their labors, for their deeds follow with them."

16:15 ("Behold, I am coming like a thief. Blessed is the one who stays awake and keeps his clothes, so that he will not walk about naked and men will not see his shame.")

19:9   Then he said to me, "Write, 'Blessed are those who are invited to the marriage supper of the Lamb.'" And he said to me, "These are true words of God."

20:6 Blessed and holy is the one who has a part in the first resurrection; over these the second death has no power, but they will be priests of God and of Christ and will reign with Him for a thousand years.

22:7 "And behold, I am coming quickly. Blessed is he who heeds the words of the prophecy of this book."

22:14   Blessed are those who wash their robes, so that they may have the right to the tree of life, and may enter by the gates into the city.

Skip Moen is the author of

*Words to Lead By*
*Spiritual Restoration, Vol. 1*
*God, Time and the Limits of Omniscience*
*Jesus Said to Her*
*Guardian Angel*
*Living In Your Zone* (with John Samuel)
*Spiritual Restoration, Vol. 2*

He has also written more than 3000 word studies which can be found on his web site

skipmoen.com